JOSHUA

in the Light of
the New Testament

D1572307

JOSHUA
in the Light of
the New Testament

The Land of Life and Rest

by

W. Graham Scroggie

KREGEL PUBLICATIONS
Grand Rapids, MI 49501

JOSHUA in the Light of the New Testament by W.
Graham Scroggie. Published by Kregel Publications
a division of Kregel, Inc. All rights reserved.

Library of Congress Cataloging in Publication Data

Scroggie, William Graham, 1877-1958.
    JOSHUA in the Light of the New Testament.

    Reprint of the 1950 ed. published by Pickering &
Inglis, London, under title: *The Land and Life of Rest.*
    1. Bible O.T. Joshua — Criticism, interpretation, etc.
— Addresses, essays, lectures. 2. Joshua, Son of Nun —
Addresses, essays, lectures. 3. Christian life —
Addresses, essays, lectures. I. Title.
BS1295.2.S35   1981   222'.20924   80-8074
ISBN 0-8254-3734-2

Printed in the United States of America

CONTENTS

INTRODUCTION

THE subject chosen for these studies is the Book of Joshua in the light of the New Testament.

But before going into the details of this book, a few words must be said about the subject in general.

In the first place, it is *life* that we are to consider. It would be to little profit if we spent time over some intellectual concept, or in the examination of some religious theory, for in the kind of world in which we are living concepts and theories fall a long way short of meeting our need. To alter for our purpose some familiar words, we may say:

> 'Tis life whereof our *souls* are scant,
> 'Tis life, not *schemes*, for which we pant,
> More life and fuller that we want.

And so we are to think about *life*. But you will observe, it is not life in general of which we speak, but a certain quality of life, the life of *rest*. Now it is of the utmost importance that we should know what this does, and does not, mean. The word 'rest' in Hebrews iv, where nearly all its occurrences in the New Testament are found, is a very interesting one. The noun means *stillness, peace, repose, tranquillity,* and the verb means to *pause,* to *stop,* to *quit,* to *desist,* to *cease,* to *refrain*; and both noun and verb have a prepositional prefix which means *thorough,* or *thoroughly.* The idea, then, is that of inward peace, of spiritual tranquillity, of complete repose, and of this state as a consequence of having *quit* something, to *cease* from it. Its significance is both negative and positive.

Further, we shall see that this life of rest is by *faith*. But what is faith? The writer to the Hebrews asks this question, and answers:

> 'It is that which gives substance to our hopes, which convinces us of things we cannot see' (Knox);

> 'It is a well-grounded assurance of that for which we hope, and a conviction of the reality of things which we do not see' (Weymouth).

Faith, then, is neither credulity nor presumption, but is a moral and spiritual principle of action, divinely given to us, if we want it (Eph. ii. 8), whereby spiritual realities are brought within the ambit of human experience. As Coleridge has said:

> 'Faith is an affirmation and an act
> That bids eternal truth be fact.'

But there is one more point of great importance, on which repeatedly we shall have to insist, namely, that this life of rest, which is by faith, is also by *effort*. The idea that we must be passive and inactive in order to live this life is contrary to the Scriptures. The truth about spiritual rest is not some mystical and mysterious conception that belongs to the realm of dream, vision, and rapturous elation, but is something which must be won and held by costly effort. The writer to the Hebrews says:

'We must *strive eagerly* to attain that rest' (iv. 11): and this word 'strive eagerly' is the same as that in Joshua iv. 10, where we read that 'the people *hasted* and passed over' the Jordan. From this we see that faith is not a substitute for effort, and that effort can never be a substitute for faith.

The truth about practical holiness has suffered at times, because it has been represented as something that needs not the effort of man for its realization. This, however, is not true. Just because we are rational and moral beings, we have some responsibility for our own sanctification.

> Rest is not quitting
>   The busy career,
> Rest is the fitting
>   Of Self to one's sphere.
>
> 'Tis loving and serving
>   The Highest and Best!
> 'Tis onwards, unswerving:
>   And that is true rest.

We are to consider, then, a quality of life which involves a forsaking and a following, and which is entered into and maintained by the faith which is trust in God, and by continuous energetic effort to translate belief into practice, to demonstrate in terms of character and conduct the truthfulness and power of one's creed.

As we approach the Book of Joshua we should recognize that the story relates to a people who already had been redeemed by blood and by power from Egyptian bondage, and who had been constituted a nation by God, that through them as His instrument He might fulfil His redeeming design for all mankind.

The fact that this book follows Exodus, Leviticus, Numbers, and Deuteronomy, determines its point of view, and shows us that the subject of it is not redemption, but the character and calling of an already redeemed people.

It is this fact which makes the book a suitable

subject for our contemplation at this time, for the
message of what is known as 'Keswick' is not addressed
to unregenerate people, though many such are reached
by it, but to us who already have had the experience
of regenerating grace, but need constantly to be confronted with the implications in life and service of
that initial blessing.   In one view, every blessing
which God has for us is given to us in the moment of
our regeneration; but in another view, all those blessings become ours only as by faith and effort we
appropriate them.

   The *inheritance,* which is the sum total of blessing,
is ours by God's gift, but the *possession* is that much of
the inheritance which we make our own.   It is this
distinction which led Joshua to say, after great ad-
vances had been made, 'there remaineth yet very
much land to be possessed' (xiii. 1).   What is enfolded
in regeneration should be unfolded in sanctification.
What is ours should become ours.   What is possible
should become actual.   What is implicit should
become explicit.   What is potential should become
potent.   In the Book of Joshua we see in the process
of becoming, what ought to be, and we see also why
much that ought to have been, never became.

   But someone may ask, 'Of what value to us to-day
can that be which took place more than twenty-three
hundred years ago?'   The answer is, that the literal
history of Israel had a typical significance.   'All these
things happened unto them by way of figure', says the
Apostle Paul.   The passover, the manna, the smitten
rock, the tabernacle, the priests, the sacrifices, the
Red Sea, and the Jordan, were all historical types of
spiritual realities; and in the Epistle to the Hebrews

it is plainly said that Canaan, and the entrance of the Israelites into it, and Joshua their leader, and the experiences of the twelve tribes in the land, all represent truths and experiences which now belong to spiritual life.

> 'If Joshua had given them rest, God would not have spoken afterward of another day. There remaineth therefore a Sabbath rest for the people of God. Let us therefore give diligence to enter into that rest, that no man fall after the same example of disobedience. We therefore who have believed do enter into that rest' (iv. 8, 9, 11, 3).

In the Book of Joshua, then, spiritual experiences are reflected in historical events; and this, not in a passage here or there, but in the entire story.

What historically was the land of rest, spiritually is the life of rest. To the Israelites the sphere of rest was a place, but to us, it is a Person, 'in Christ in heavenly places' (Eph. i. 3). Christ is our inheritance, as Canaan was theirs, and our appropriation of the Lord is the antitype of their possession of the land. The sphere of the Israelites was earthly, but the believer's sphere is heavenly. Their sphere had boundaries, but ours has none. Their enrichment was temporary, but ours is eternal.

What is presented historically in Joshua is set forth spiritually in the Epistles, and what of old was the portion of one nation, is now the privilege of the universal Church of God.

Let us now look briefly at the scope of that which we are to study.

The Book of Joshua is in three unequal but vitally

related parts. The titles of these parts are, *Entering the Land* (chs. i. 1-v. 12); *Conquering the Land* (chs. v. 13-xii. 24); and *Possessing the Land* (chs. xiii-xxiv).

These titles indicate not only the course of the history, but also reveal the spiritual truth which the history enfolds. The spiritual blessing which the history typifies must be *entered* by an act of faith. That is the subject of part one. Then, the land which we have entered must be fought for; our enemies must be *conquered;* faith must be backed up by effort. That is the subject of part two. And finally, the land which has been entered and fought for, must be *possessed;* faith and effort will lead to great enrichment. That is the subject of part three.

The order is progressive. *Entrance* must precede *conquest,* and conquest must precede *possession.* If it be thought strange that we must fight to rest, it is worthy of our notice that the Epistle to the Ephesians, which is the New Testament counterpart of the Book of Joshua, emphatically connects rest with conflict. There it is said that we are 'blessed with all spiritual blessings in the heavenlies in Christ', that we are 'made to sit together in the heavenlies in Christ Jesus', and that it is there, 'in the heavenlies', that we are to 'wrestle against principalities, against powers, against the rulers of the darkness of this world, against spiritual wickedness' (i. 3; ii. 6; vi. 12). This expression, 'the heavenlies', which occurs five times in Ephesians, has well been defined as 'the sphere of the believer's spiritual experience as identified with Christ' (Scofield). It is the New Testament equivalent of the land in Joshua. We shall understand this if we keep clearly before us two things; firstly, what every Christian is and has in Christ, from the moment of his conversion; and secondly, what every Christian should become and have in Christ by faith and effort. The first relates to our spiritual standing in Christ, and the second, to our actual state experimentally. Unless this distinction is kept in view our thinking will be foggy, and our endeavours disappointing. The entering, and conquering, and possessing, are the translating into experience of all the blessings which are already ours in Christ.

1

ENTERING THE LAND

Joshua 1:1-5:12

IN the first part of this Book of Joshua, that which treats of *Entering the Land,* the central feature is the Jordan, and in relation to it three distinct movements are discernible:

first, to the River, Joshua 1-2
second, through the River, Joshua 3-4
third, from the River, Joshua 5:1-12

The first tells of the *Preparation* to cross; the second, of the *Passage* across; and the third, of *Purification* after having crossed.

Let us look first of all at

THE PREPARATION TO CROSS THE RIVER (Chs. 1-2)

This preparation is *inward* in ch. i, and *outward* in ch. ii. The one reveals *faith in principle;* and the other exhibits *faith in practice;* and these emphasize the relation to one another of creed and conduct.

In the inward preparation we should observe that *divine blessings are promised,* and *human conditions are imposed.*

The blessings promised are: *the land as a sphere of life,* the gift of God to His people (2-4); *victory over all foes* (5, 8); and *the comradeship of God Himself,* all the way and all the time (9).

But these are not unconditional promises. Privilege always involves obligation, and so the responsibility of Joshua and the people is made plain. The conditions imposed are: *knowledge* of the will of God as revealed in His Word (8); *obedience* to all that God requires (8); and dauntless *courage* at all times (6, 7, 9, 18).

These promises and conditions are the roots of the Christian life, and are the secrets of all spiritual progress, and must be apprehended by the faith which is trust in God.

God calls us to a sphere of life, tells us that we can live triumphantly in it, and assures us of His presence and help. But if all this is to become experimental, it must be met by knowledge, obedience, and courage. The life of rest has deep foundations, apart from which there can *be* no rest.

But we have already said that faith as a principle of action is not enough for the realization of God's will for us; there must also be the action; only by faith *and* action can we experimentally enter the land, conquer our foes, and possess our inheritance; and so in chapter ii, we see put into action the faith of chapter i. It is true that 'God worketh in us', but we must 'work out' the salvation which He 'works in' (Phil. ii. 12, 13).

We may rely on God to do for us what we cannot do for ourselves, but we may not rely on Him to do for us what we ourselves are capable of doing. To expect God to give us help and direction without our employing the means which He has placed within our reach, is not faith, but presumption; it is not trust, but trifling.

There is no victory without struggle; there is no perfection without perseverance. If we would triumph

we must try; if we would win we must fight.
There is a professed reliance upon the Holy Spirit
which is just ignorance and indolence. Sun, and rain,
and the virtues of the soil could not in ten thousand
years produce a harvest if man did not sow seed; and
having sown seed, the harvest can be of no use to him
unless he reaps it.

God had said to Joshua, 'I give to the children of
Israel the land', but in the same breath He said,
'Every place that the soles of your feet shall tread
upon shall be yours' (i. 2, 3; Deut. xi. 24). The feet
must answer to the faith. It is of no use indolently
to dream about the goal; we must energetically foot
the track.

As Joshua sent men to discover the wealth of the land
and the strength of the foe, so we, by all available
means, should learn how great is our inheritance in
Christ, and the nature and strength of the foes and
forces which would prevent our possessing it. As the
first word should always be *God,* the second should
always be *go.*

We should always be preparing for circumstances
that will arise, and for blessings that are to come,
without foreseeing what these circumstances and
blessings will be. This preparation consists in attention to present duty, and acceptance of present disci-
pline. If day by day we first seek divine direction,
and then follow it, we shall be ready, when new circumstances arise, for the new blessings which will be
offered. To-day should be a preparation for to-
morrow. The only proof that we shall be equal to
to-morrow's test is that we are meeting to-day's test
believingly and courageously. The only evidence

that we shall be willing for God's will to-morrow is that we are subject to His will to-day.

Faith and action constituted the preparation of Israel to enter the promised land; faith in God, and sensible effort; and not otherwise shall we enter into 'that rest' of which the writer to the Hebrews speaks.

Some of our hymns expose themselves to criticism in this matter by laying emphasis on what, at most, is but half a truth.   One hymn says, 'Doing is a deadly thing, doing ends in death.'   If by that is meant that effort alone cannot save us, it is true; but if it means that faith is enough, without effort, then it is not true; and James would reply, 'Shew me thy faith apart from thy works, and I by my works will shew thee my faith' (Jas. ii. 18).

JOSHUA 1:1-5:12

Another hymn says:

> I struggled and wrestled to win it,
>   The blessing that setteth me free;
> But when I had ceased from my struggles,
>   His peace Jesus gave unto me.

That is true only as 'struggling and wrestling' are regarded apart from faith; but given faith, the New Testament bids us to fight and wrestle, tells us what foes we are to engage, and what provision is made for the conflict (Eph. vi. 10-18).

I have laid emphasis on this two-fold aspect of truth, because it has been charged against 'Keswick' that it teaches quietism, a mystical and passive subordination of the will; but I do not hesitate to say that that criticism is contrary to fact.   Let it be definitely said that those who would enter into the experience of a richer and fuller life, have something *to do* as well as something *to believe*.

Now let us come to the second movement in this part of our subject.

The Passage Through the River (Chs. 3-4)

Here let us consider the meaning of the River; the distinction, typically, between the Red Sea and the River; and the spiritual teaching of this crossing of the River.

As to the meaning of the River, again we must be warned that our hymns do not always rightly interpret the Scriptures, and the matter before us is a case in point.   There is a hymn that says:

> Why should I shrink at pain and woe,
>   Or feel, at death, dismay?
> I've Canaan's goodly land in view,
>   And realms of endless day.

But what is there said suggestively is, in another hymn, and by a better-known writer, said emphatically. Speaking of heaven, he says:

> Death like a narrow sea divides
> This heavenly land from ours.

And he continues:

> Sweet fields beyond the swelling flood
>   Stand dressed in living green;
> So to the Jews old Canaan stood,
>   While Jordan rolled between.

> But timorous mortals start and shrink
>   To cross the narrow sea,
> And linger, shrinking at the brink,
>   And fear to launch away.

> O could we make our doubts remove
>   Those gloomy thoughts that rise,
> And see the Canaan that we love
>   With unbeclouded eyes;
>
> Could we but climb where Moses stood,
>   And view the landscape o'er,
> Not Jordan's stream, nor death's cold flood,
>   Should fright us from the shore.

That is not worthy of the man who wrote:

> When I survey the wondrous Cross
>   On which the Prince of glory died.

In these hymns the Jordan is taken to represent death, and Canaan, to represent heaven. If that were so, heaven would lose much of its attractiveness for some of us, for to pursue the illustration, the first thing we would have to do on arriving would be to start a vigorous fight; and what is worse, if this representation were true, we would take into heaven all our faults and failings, to perpetuate there, what we bemoan here.

Surely it is clear that some other interpretation must be looked for, more consistent with the whole story; and to distinguish between the significance of the Red Sea and the Jordan may give us a clue.

If we believe that the history of Israel is typical, then their passage, first through the Red Sea, and then through the Jordan, must have spiritual significance. The order of these passages is important, first the Red Sea, and then the Jordan, and but for the former there could never have been the latter. Historically and geographically the order could not have been inverted, and spiritually it cannot be.

By the passage through the Red Sea the people

were separated from a life of bondage in Egypt, and
by the passage through the Jordan they were dedicated
to a life of blessing in Canaan. The first experience
was *from* something, and the second, was *to* something.
In the one case something lay behind them to which
they could never return, and in the other case something lay before them towards which they pressed.
The Sea was a way of exit, and the River was a way
of entrance.

Now this is precisely the order in spiritual experience.
We must have a Red Sea experience before we can
have a Jordan experience, though time is not a factor
here. In the history, forty years lay between the two
events, but in spiritual experience they may be, and
should be, simultaneous, though, alas, too often they
are separated by varying lengths of time.

Yet, that which these events signify—a *deliverance
from,* and a *dedication to*—must be distinguished by us
in apprehension and appropriation. The significance
of the River is *enfolded* in the Sea, and the significance
of the Sea is *unfolded* at the River; just as the five
offerings are enfolded in, and are an unfolding of,
the passover.

What, then, is the spiritual teaching of this crossing
of the River?

Much emphasis is laid upon it in the New Testament, as, for example, in Gal. ii. 20:

> 'I have been crucified with Christ; yet I live;
> And yet no longer I, but Christ liveth in me.':

and in Col. ii. 20; iii. 1:

> 'Ye died with Christ'.
> 'Ye were raised together with Christ':

and especially in Rom. vi. 1-11; in which the words occur:

> 'Baptized into Christ's death.'
>
> 'Buried with Him into death.'
>
> 'United with Him by the likeness of His death.'
>
> '(United with Him) also by the likeness of His resurrection.'
>
> 'If we died with Christ, we believe that we shall also live with Him.'
>
> 'Reckon ye yourselves to be dead unto sin, but alive unto God in Christ Jesus.'

The teaching of these passages is that in Christ's death the believer died, and in His resurrection the believer was raised to live a new life. The profoundest truth of the New Testament is that which declares that the death, burial, and resurrection of Christ indicate what happens to the individual who trusts Him for salvation.

If you are a Christian, this is not something that can happen now, but is something that did happen in the hour of your regeneration, afterwards to be apprehended and reckoned upon. It is nothing that we can do, but is something that has been done; which the believer should accept by faith, and to the implications of which he should commit himself wholeheartedly.

The history illustrates this profound truth by two facts. First, by the fact that the ark, which represents Christ, was the first to go into the Jordan, and the last to come out of it (iii. 17; iv. 11), for Christ is the Alpha and Omega of salvation, 'the leader and completer of faith' (Heb. xii. 2). And secondly, by the fact that

JOSHUA 1:1-5:12

twelve memorial stones were placed 'in the midst of Jordan' (iv. 9), soon to be submerged by the returning waters; and twelve were placed on the west side of Jordan (iv. 4-8), to be a perpetual witness to the miraculous passage through the River. The memorial in the Jordan tells of *death,* and the memorial over Jordan tells of *resurrection;* truths which are summarized in the apostolic words,

'Ye died, and your life is hid with Christ in God' (Col. iii. 3).

If the Red Sea passage typifies God's judgment on *sin,* the Jordan passage typifies His judgment on *self.* The Christian is not an old self renovated, but crucified; one who has had a new self imparted and implanted. Perhaps the last truth which we are willing to believe and act upon, is that our natural self was put to death on the Cross, and must continuously be regarded as in the place of death.

The things in our experience which we regret and deplore, or should do, are activities of the old nature; but we are exhorted to

'reckon ourselves to be dead unto sin,
    and alive unto God in Christ Jesus' (Rom. vi. 11).

Soul of mine, must I surrender,
    See myself the crucified,
Turn from all of earth's ambition
    That thou may'st be satisfied?

Yes, that is what is required, and in no other way can one experience the rest which is inward peace.

God views the believer as dead and risen in Christ, but it constitutes a crisis in spiritual experience when the believer comes to view himself in this way. To multitudes there once came an hour when by faith they 'passed clean over Jordan'; an hour when they came to recognize and to reckon upon what, by Christ's death and resurrection, is already accomplished, namely, that they 'died', and that their 'life is hid with Christ in God' (Col. iii. 3).

We are not to try to die, but to reckon upon death as a fact. I have already quoted, 'reckon ye your-selves to be dead unto sin' (Rom. vi. 11). Here some-one may say, 'but self in me is not dead, so how can I reckon it to be?' That line of reasoning does not take in the whole truth. Think, for illustration, of a man condemned to death for murder, waiting in his cell for the execution of the sentence. Two things are true of him; first, that he is dead; and second, that he is not dead. In the view of the law he died when sentence was pronounced upon him, and he will actually die when that sentence is executed. In his cell the condemned man is robbed of liberty, of all rights and privileges, and of his existence as a member of society. By his sin he has forfeited all this, and so his is a living death until he goes to the gallows.

In like manner, by dying, Christ condemned sinful self to death, so that in the believer that self is under sentence of death, robbed of all rights, and awaiting only the day of decease, or of Christ's return, when it will be finally eliminated. This is how we are to 'reckon' our sinful self to be 'dead'.

But the Christian is denying this fact and truth, who claims the right to think, and say, and do what he likes. The experience of Christians is often a sad thing, but Christian experience is making true in daily

life that which is already true of us in Christ Jesus.
Well did John Wesley say:

> Frames and feelings fluctuate:
>   These can ne'er thy saviour be!
> Learn thyself in Christ to see:
>   Then, be feelings what they will,
>   Jesus is thy Saviour still.

The apostle does not tell us in Rom. vi. 11 to reckon
sin dead, but to reckon ourselves dead to it, and Godet
appreciates this distinction when he says:

> 'the Christian's breaking with sin is undoubtedly
> gradual in its realization, but absolute and con-
> clusive in its principle. To break with sin there is
> indeed a decisive and radical act, a divine deed
> taking possession of the soul, and interposing
> henceforth between the will of the believer and sin.'

By Christ crucified and risen we are crucified 'unto
the world' (Gal. vi. 14); and, as an old puritan has
said: 'though corruption is not ejected from its in-
herency, it is, by Christ, dejected from its regency.'

This, then, is the teaching of the passage through
the Jordan.

There remains one more movement in this part of
our study. We have considered the preparation to
cross the River, and the passage through the River,
and now there is

THE PURIFICATION BEYOND THE RIVER (Ch. v. 1-12).

Two things here claim our attention: the circumcision of the new generation of Israelites at Gilgal;
and the new fare at the old feast.

On the west of the River the first encampment of

the Israelites was at Gilgal, a name which means *the rolling away of reproach*. All the males who had been born in the wilderness were uncircumcized, and as soon as the Jordan was crossed the Lord commanded Joshua to circumcize them; which, of course, he did.

The attention which is given to this matter in the record indicates its importance, and the references both to Gilgal and circumcision, here and in other Scriptures, sufficiently indicate the spiritual significance of the event (ch. v. 1-9).

It is impressive that the Apostle Paul after saying, 'ye died, and your life is hid with Christ in God', continues, 'mortify therefore your members which are upon the earth' (Col. iii. 3, 5). This word 'mortify' means, *put to death, deprive of power, render impotent.*

Now this may seem to contradict what has already been said, namely, that in Christ's death, we died; for if this be so, it may well be asked, what is there left to be put to death? At the risk, therefore, of some repetition, let it be said again that the teaching of the Epistles distinguishes between what, by divine grace, we are in Christ by virtue of His death and resurrection, and what experimentally we may and should become by faith and effort in the energy of the Holy Spirit. In other words, there is in thought, and too often and too largely in fact, a difference between our spiritual standing, and our spiritual state.

This truth is expressed clearly in 1 Corinthians v. 7, which says:

> 'Get rid of the old yeast so that you may be dough of a new kind; for in fact you are free from corruption.' (Weymouth).

What in effect this passage says is, *become what you*

are; and therein is the whole philosophy of the Christian life. We should die because we are dead; we should live because we are alive; we should conquer because we have won. To quote the couplet again:

> Faith is an affirmation and an act
> That bids eternal truth be fact.

What we should recognize is the *fact*, and that recognition will lead us to *act*. And so, as Paul says, because 'we died', we should 'put to death' those passions in us which belong to earth (Knox), our earthward inclinations (Weymouth); that is, *we should achieve the accomplished.*

This is the significance of the operation at Gilgal. The Israelites had entered into a new experience; they had exchanged the wilderness for the land, and they were called upon in the first place to act upon the known will of God, by putting away all cause of reproach.

Here it is necessary to point out that in the experience which the history typifies, the events are not consecutive, but contemporaneous. It is psychologically unsound to tabulate an order of spiritual experiences which the believer should follow. So many things happen simultaneously as to make distinctions possible only in thought.

As in regeneration there are not separate moments of justification, forgiveness, and sonship, so in sanctification there are not separate moments of yielding, of cleansing, and of the infilling of the Spirit. But though we cannot regiment spiritual experience in that way, we should endeavour to see what are the factors which enter into and constitute the more abundant life.

The last thing in this part of our study relates to *the old feast and the new fare* (v. 10-12). We read that, after the operation of circumcision, the children of Israel kept the passover. This feast had not been observed once during the thirty-eight years of wandering in the wilderness; but that being ended, it is again observed. Spiritual revival always unveils the Cross afresh.

But what distinguished this passover from all others that had previously been observed, is that from then 'the manna ceased', and the people ate of 'the old corn of the land'. The manna had come down, but the corn came up; and as Christ is the Bread of Life it is not difficult to see Him here in two aspects, first as incarnate, coming down from heaven, and then as risen from the dead, to be the sustenance of His people. In the history 'the manna ceased' when the Israelites entered the land, but in the spiritual counterpart we cannot separate the manna from the corn, we cannot separate the incarnate from the risen Christ, for it is the whole Christ, incarnate, living, crucified, and living again, Who is the food of His people.

We cannot think too much of the crucifixion, but we can and do think sadly too little of the resurrection, the resurrection which is not only a historical event, but also a spiritual power and experience. Life in the land represents ideally our living in the power of our risen Lord.

JOSHUA 1:1-5:12

> Lord Jesus, are we one with Thee!
>   Oh height, oh depth of love!
> Thou, one with us upon the tree,
>   We, one with Thee above!

This, then, is the message of the first part of the Book of Joshua.   While we are in this world we cannot cease to be 'strangers and pilgrims', but we should cease to be sinful wanderers.

There is an experience which is spoken of as 'rest', to which the children of God are entitled and enjoined, and it is something other than and after regeneration.   When our Lord said (John x. 10): 'I came that they may have life', surely He referred to regeneration; and when He added: 'and have it abundantly', surely He referred to the entire experience of which we have been speaking; and surely our being here at this time is for this purpose.

I will conclude with some words written by Evan Hopkins, and set to music by Handley Moule, men of blessed memory at Keswick, who, though dead, are yet speaking, inviting us all to claim and enter into 'the peace of God which passeth all understanding'. Let us make these words the sincere prayer of our hearts now.

> My Saviour, Thou hast offered rest;
>   Oh, give it then to me;
> The rest of ceasing from myself,
>   To find my all in Thee.
>
> O Lord, I seek a holy rest,
>   A victory over sin;
> I seek that Thou alone shouldst reign
>   O'er all without, within.

2

CONQUERING THE LAND
Joshua 5:13-12:24

BEFORE the land of Canaan could be *possessed* by the Israelites it had to be *conquered;* and before it could be conquered it had to be *entered.*

The subject of *Entering the Land* we have considered both historically and spiritually. What to the Israelite was a *land* is to the Christian a *life;* and the *preparation,* the *passage,* and the *purification* in the history, have their counterparts, we have seen, in spiritual truths and experiences which belong exclusively to the Christian revelation, and to the Christian.

But all this is for us, as it was for Israel, only the beginning of an unfolding divine purpose, and we must be careful not to regard the means as the end.

We now come to the second of the three divisions of the Book of Joshua, that which tells of Israel *Conquering the Land.* And here three things claim our purposeful attention: *the revelation of the Captain* (ch. v. 13-15); *the record of the conflict* (chs. vi-xi); and *the review of the conquest* (ch. xii).

First, then, is:

THE REVELATION OF THE CAPTAIN (Ch. 5:13-15)

And the first thing to consider here is, *the time of the revelation.*

The land had been entered, and the people were now encamped between the Jordan and Jericho. The one rendered impossible their retreat, and the

other challenged their advance. It was for them a
solemn and serious situation; but all they had been
told to do they had done; the sons had been circum-
cized, and the passover had been observed; and
Joshua now awaited further divine direction.

No doubt we shall in days to come, as in the past,
find ourselves in difficult situations and circumstances, and it will be well for us if at such times we
have a conscience void of offence, if we are sure that,
so far as we know, we have done the will of God; for
if we have not that assurance we are not ready for any
fresh revelation, nor are we ready for any further
advance. Fresh light is given only to the obedient;
and direction in the way is given only to those who
have faithfully followed past guidance.

In the next place consider *the nature of the revelation.*

Joshua was alone, prayerfully contemplating what
the next step should be, when suddenly there appeared
before him 'a man, with his sword drawn in his hand'.
Joshua challenged him; 'Art thou for us, or for our
adversaries?' and got for reply: 'I, the Captain of the
LORD's host, have now come'.

This was an event of profound importance, and the
following four points should be carefully considered:
that the man who appeared was a warrior; that
Joshua was prepared to fight; that Joshua knew of only
two sides, 'for', and 'against'; and that the man
warrior announced that He was more than man;
that He was none other than the Captain of all God's
angelic hosts; and that for the conflict now about to
begin, He had come, not merely to direct the army of
Israel, but to fight for and with it.

Now every part of this incident is relevant to the Church of God, and to the individual Christian. God in Christ appears in many aspects to His people, and always in the manner most suited to the circumstances and need of the hour.

To Jacob He came as a wrestler; to Moses He appeared 'in a flame of fire'; to Joshua He reveals Himself as a warrior; to the afflicted He is the God of comfort; to the depressed He is the God of hope; to the lonely He is a friend; to the storm-tossed He is an anchor; and to the longing soul He is the Lord Who meets our every need; and in all these and many other aspects He is here to-day, because our needs are manifold.

JOSHUA 5:13-12:24

And now, look for a moment at *the effect of the revelation.*

The man who was first anxious, and then brave, is now worshipful and obedient. He recognized in that 'man' before him the divine LORD; and when He said, 'I am now come', Joshua knew that He had come to give the Israelites victory over all their foes.

This manifestation of the LORD, and in such a setting, makes it abundantly clear that the *rest* of which this Book speaks, and of which it is a prophecy, is something that comes, not by indolence, but by action; not by faith only, but also by strenuous effort.

The figures which the New Testament presents of the Christian life are such as always indicate, not strain, but strenuousness, effort, energy, figures such as racing, boxing, and fighting to withstand the forces of evil. The life to which we are called is not a glorified picnic, but a warfare, and our divine Gideon has no use for those who dread, and those who delay, but only for those who dare. It may be pleasing to the flesh to linger by the brook, but Christ calls us to the battle.

A young man who attended a Convention for the promotion of holiness and was blessed, on returning to his home in Edinburgh went to see his minister, Dr. Alexander Whyte, and gave him the impression that he imagined his troubles were now at an end. The aged saint listened to him patiently, and then said to him quietly: 'My boy, you'll find that it will be a sair fecht to the end'.

Was he not right? The way of the fully yielded life is not one of escapism, but is one of conflict issuing in victory; the life of rest is a life of unceasing action and boundless energy. The idea of being carried to heaven on 'flowery beds of ease', is not a revelation, but the raving of a lazy dreamer. The Spirit says, 'Put on the whole armour of God'.

Immediately following this revelation of the Captain comes

THE RECORD OF THE CONFLICT (Chs. 6-11)

Viewing this division as a whole, we should see clearly that *the land of rest was a land of conflict,* and that *the life of rest is a life of conflict.* We have insisted on this, because the Scriptures insist on it. The true Christian is not morally and spiritually flabby and anæmic, but robust and energetic, and because there is so much in this world that should be resisted, he is an indefatigable resister, an inveterate nonconformist.

Then, let us understand that now spiritually, as then historically, *the Canaan conflict is a great campaign.* A *battle* is a single engagement, but a *campaign* is a series of concerted military operations directed towards a a single objective. The sooner we get this campaign view of life the better, because it gives unity to all events and experiences. Were life-issues determined by a single battle, and we lost that battle, how terrible it would be for us all. But this is not so. We may lose battles, and yet win the campaign.

And this view of life not only unifies the experiences of each of us, but it unites all Christians in a common objective, for a campaign cannot be fought by an individual. It was not Joshua that conquered Canaan, but all Israel, and the conflict throughout the Christian dispensation is not the responsibility of a few individuals, however distinguished, but of the whole Church of God.

And another factor here relates to *time*. The Christian campaign is coextensive with the Christian dispensation. The conflict in which we are engaged is that in which all believers have been engaged for nearly two thousand years. Our armour is that which was worn by Paul, and Athanasius, and Augustine, and Bunyan, and Calvin, and Luther, and Wesley, and Spurgeon, and the uncountable millions who have served with the great leaders. Not without good reason did John Bunyan call his great allegory *The Holy War;* and not without equally good reason did William Gurnall call his great work on Ephesians vi. 10-20—a work of over 820 closely-printed pages— *The Christian in Complete Armour,* or *A Treatise on the Saints' War with the Devil.* We speak of *the Church militant,* but is the Church as righteously combative as it used to be? There is no cessation of the Christian

JOSHUA 5:13-12:24

Campaign, and each of us is either a soldier or a skunk.

Another thing in this overall view of the conflict is that *because Christ is the Captain victory is assured ultimately*. Our divine Joshua cannot fail, though we may fail Him. 'Thine is the kingdom, and the power, and the glory'. Then

> Fight the good fight with all thy might;
> Christ is thy strength, and Christ thy right;
> Lay hold on life, and it shall be
> Thy joy and crown eternally.

Now we must consider in detail the great conflict, then and now.

And the first thing to observe is that the conflict, as I have said, was and is *a campaign,* that is, an organised course of action. The campaigns of Alexander, and Napoleon, and more recent ones, were not un-intelligent and unorganized mob assaults here and there, in the hope of gaining some military advantage, but carefully planned, and as carefully executed, efforts to reach some clearly defined objective.

The devil is not such a fool as to engage in wild mêlées, and confused scuffles and skirmishes, in his efforts to extend and establish his kingdom; for by his 'devices', of which we read in 2 Cor. ii. 11, is meant his carefully thought-out strategies, his adaptation of means to ends, an illustration of which we have in his temptation of Jesus in the wilderness.

And when we examine this division in the Book of Joshua, we see that the conflicts of the Israelites were not desultory battles, but a carefully organized campaign. The strategy was to drive a wedge into the centre of the land, westward from Jericho, and in this way to separate the foes in the south from those in the north, thus preventing them from uniting to make a mass assault on the Israelites (chs. vi—ix). After that, the army turned south and dealt with the enemy there (ch. x), and then went north to complete the plan (ch. xi).

In warfare almost everything depends on strategy, on such a movement of troops, or ships, or planes as to impose upon the enemy the place, and time, and conditions for fighting proffered by oneself; and if such tactics are necessary in worldly warfare, do we suppose that we can dispense with them in the spiritual realm, in the age-long conflict of right with wrong, of truth with error, of holiness with sin? Yet, is it not true that it is here we think least of generalship, strategy, tactics, plan, call it what you like, and so at every turn we are outmanœuvred by the *methodeias,* the artifices, the wiles of the devil (Eph. vi. 11; iv. 14, Gr.).

May it not be that here lies the explanation of those defeats and failures which we so deplore, and which we have come to think of, perhaps, as inevitable. If we have been fighting on the hit-or-miss method, if it can be called a method, it is little wonder that we have more often missed than hit.

The next thing to observe is that at each stage of the campaign in Canaan there was *a critical battle;* and we have seen that there were three such stages, the central, the southern, and the northern, in each of which success or failure depended largely on what was done at one, or at most, two places.

At the first stage the two critical places were Jericho and Ai (chs. vi—viii); at the second stage, they were Gibeon and Beth-horon (ch. x); and at the third stage, it was at the waters of Merom (ch. xi). No doubt during the campaign, which occupied about seven years, many battles were fought, but the historian records only those which determined the issue of the campaign. We shall return to the details of these engagements later, but let us look for a moment at the main fact as it affects ourselves.

In our spiritual life the importance of battles is relative. Of course all are important, but some are of supreme importance, as were the engagements at Jericho, Ai, Gibeon, Beth-horon, and Merom. Every event in our life has some importance, but some events are vital and crucial. What we do at one point may be decisive for a wide area; one critical choice may determine many minor choices. Many of these crucial and decisive battles have been fought by tens of thousands of people, and many, no doubt, will be fought by thousands more.

Opportunities involve obligations; privileges imply responsibilities, and so we are all confronted with the necessity of relating ourselves in some way to the challenge of God's Word, and the claim of Christ.

Every battle is either lost, drawn, or won. Lost battles are depressing; drawn battles are enervating; but won battles are inspiring. To lose is tragical; to draw is dangerous; but we can win if we will to.

Now let us look at the details of the conflict in Canaan, and learn what they have to teach us.

First of all we shall take *the central conflict* (chs. vi— ix), and learn what we may about the secrets of victory, and the causes of defeat.

The Secrets of Victory are various, but are vitally

related, and they are exhibited, in the story, in Israel's advance on Jericho. For a moment or two let us contemplate three of them, *faith, obedience,* and *courage.* You will find all these in ch. vi.

First of all there is *faith,* and it is this to which the writer to the Hebrews calls attention: 'by faith the walls of Jericho fell down, after they were compassed about seven days' (Heb. xi. 30).

Faith is difficult to define, but confidence in and reliance upon Almighty God is of its essence. And just because it is this, the unchristian world, and worldly Christians cannot understand it; in their view faith is folly; and, let it be admitted, those who exercise it are sometimes made to look very foolish.

Take the case of the siege of Jericho. Could anything on earth be more utterly ridiculous? First there were the armed men; then seven white-robed priests, blowing discordant ram's horn trumpets; then the ark; and finally the people. For six days this crowd circumambulated Jericho in complete silence, except for the ram's horns, and then returned to their base. No doubt during the two hours which this performance may have lasted, the people of Jericho assembled on the walls above, and laughed at the absurd exhibition. Then, on the seventh day, which probably was a Sabbath, the procession compassed the city seven times instead of once, and at the end of the seventh circuit the people, at Joshua's command, gave a fierce yell, and down came the walls of the city in ruinous confusion, and the host marched in and took possession.

Things like that have not happened in our time, but the same dauntless faith has been displayed in other patterns; as, for example, when martyrs, men and women, bravely went to rack, and flame, and arena of wild beasts, rather than deny the Lord who had saved them. To such stalwart faith in God we are all called, and it is the only hope of our bankrupt world. We, the least of us, have the opportunity to make history glorious. 'This is the victory that overcometh the world, our faith' (1 John v. 4).

The second secret of victory is *obedience*. This is vitally related to *faith*, and it is spoken of by Paul as 'the obedience of faith'.

Let us not imagine that it was easy for the Israelites to do as they were told. On each of six days they were told to march once and silently round the walls of Jericho, and then return to their base. They were not told why they had to do this, nor what was to happen in consequence. The procedure must have seemed quite absurd, but they were told by God, through Joshua, to do this, and so they did it, and not until the seventh day were they told what more to do, and what the end of it all would be.

To the worldling all this is irrational and unbelievable, but to those who have faith there is no alternative to obedience. If we believe that the will of God is 'good, and acceptable, and perfect', and if we genuinely put our trust in Him, the only rational thing to do is to obey Him. Christian obedience is not based on knowledge, but on faith. Rarely, if ever, does God interpret His commands in advance, for if He did, faith would lose more than half its opportunity. When He tells us what to do, it is not for us to make reply, it is not for us to reason why, but simply, though blindly, to do.

This is what Abraham did when he left Chaldea, and when he went to Mount Moriah. This is what Moses did when he took two slabs of stone up into Mount Sinai. This is what Elijah did when God told him to go where he would be fed by ravens. And this is what God expects you and me to do when He calls us; for 'all the steps,' and all the stops, 'of a godly man are ordered by the Lord'. Our salvation is based on faith, but our sanctification is based on obedience. All regenerated persons are God's children, but all are not His friends, for it is written: 'ye are My friends if ye *do* whatsoever I command you'.

The third secret of victory which this story discloses is *courage*. Courage is fearlessness, bravery, boldness, and it is of various kinds, physical, intellectual, moral, and spiritual. To be a true Christian one must have the courage of his convictions, for of what use are convictions where there is no courage?

Some public expressions of religious fervour are not necessarily evidences of courage; they may be simply priggish; but to live a simple, humble, sincere Christian life in the home, the hospital, the office, the shop; at school, at college, at the club, and wherever one may be, will require not a little courage in these days of crass selfishness, and crumbling morality. Dead fish always go with the current, but luscious salmon breast it.

Without these qualities—faith, obedience, and courage—one cannot hope for success in the Christian life; but with them, one will neither fear nor fall.

And now let us consider the *Causes of Defeat*, for the next part of the story tells of defeat. The fact that

JOSHUA 5:13-12:24

this is so is solemn and significant. Just as after the Book of Joshua comes the Book of Judges, so after Jericho came Ai, after victory came defeat. Let us believe at once that the experience of victory may blind us to the possibility of defeat. Heights are dangerous places. Only a steady hand can carry a full cup. In Jesus' experience, after the Dove came the devil; after the divine attestation came the diabolical attack; and can we suppose that it will be otherwise with ourselves?

In fact, as in name, Ai was a much smaller place than Jericho, though, as we shall see, it was not less important in the unfolding plan. As we read in ch. vii the story of Israel's first fight and first failure, we shall see that there were in the main, two causes of defeat: *self-confidence*, and *covetousness;* and these are still prime causes of failure in a Christian's life.

First then, *self-confidence* was a cause of defeat (ch. vii. 2-5).

Spies were sent from Jericho to Ai to view the situation there, and report. The advice they gave on their return was followed immediately and without question. It was:

> 'Let not all the people go up; but let about two or three thousand men go up and smite Ai; and make not all the people to labour thither; for they are but few' (3).

It will be seen at once that this was a wrong standard of judgment, and dearly did the army pay for following it. The centre of gravity had shifted from the Divine to the human; from spiritual might to fleshly mathematics. The point is not that more soldiers would ensure victory. So far from this being the case,

Gideon was told that he would have to get rid of most
of his army if he would defeat the Midianites (Judg.
vii. 2). What mattered, and matters, is that they
and we trust completely in God, and do our
utmost. Joshua did neither of these things at this
time, and so Israel suffered defeat. This self-confidence was not the expression of considered and
deliberate sin, but was due to thoughtlessness and
prayerlessness.

'We take scant pains about what we think easy
work', yet we can never afford to treat the enemy with
contempt. There are no occasions on which we are
able to win battles without the help of God.

Self-confidence is simply making self the centre and
circumference of one's confidence, and this is a denial
of Christ and Christianity. Peter said that though
all the Apostles denied the Lord, he never would;
yet he was the only one of them who did.

In the second place *covetousness*, leading to ir-
religion and immorality (vii. 11), was, and is, a cause
of defeat (vii. 1, 11-13, 21).

Achan, a member of the camp, took some of the
spoil from Jericho, 'a Babylonish garment, two
hundred shekels of silver, and a wedge of gold of fifty
shekels' weight', and hid it in his tent.

The sin of this was twofold; *he took what was forbidden*, and in doing so, *he robbed God* (ch. vi. 17-19,
marg.), and the root of both sins was covetousness.
Achan himself gives the history of this evil; he said: 'I
saw, I *coveted*, I *took*, I *hid*' (ch. vii. 21). This followed
the pattern of the first sin: 'the woman *saw*, and *desired*,
and *took*, and did *eat*, and *gave*' (Gen. iii. 6); and it is
the normal pattern of every sin, as the stories of Lot,

and Samson, and David, and Judas, and others show.

The genealogy and psychology of this evil is given in a weighty passage:

> 'Each person is tempted when he is lured and enticed by his own desire. Then desire, when it has conceived gives birth to sin; and sin, when it is full-grown, brings forth death' (Jas. i. 14, 15).

It is not a sin to be tempted, but it is a sin to yield. 'The outward object has no power to make us fall except as it corresponds to an inward affection'. The curse of the world from the beginning is found largely in two things; in seeking out the hidden, and taking the forbidden; in yielding to curiosity and covetousness.

Now this is bad enough in the individual, but it never ends there. No one can live to himself, and no one can sin to himself. As a drop of poison does not remain at the point of injection, but affects the whole body, so when we sin we injure not ourselves only, but other people also. All Israel suffered because Achan sinned. What the Lord said to Joshua is both strange and solemn:

> '*Israel* has sinned, and they have also transgressed my covenant which I commanded them: for they have even taken of the accursed thing, and have also stolen, and dissembled also, and they have put it, even among their own stuff.
>
> Therefore the *children of Israel* could not stand before their enemies, but turned their backs before their enemies, because they were accursed; neither will I be with you any more, except ye destroy the accursed thing from among you' (ch. vii. 11, 12).

It was Achan only that had done this, yet it was

attributed to Israel, and Israel was held responsible; but when Achan was convicted, it was he and not Israel that died.

It is true, of course, that a man's sin is his own, but it is equally true that it does not terminate in himself. In that Psalm of sobs, the 51st, David says: 'I did it; yes, I did it'; but we know that the consequences followed in his family; and we have echoes of it to-day, three thousand years after the event (2 Sam. xii).

JOSHUA 5:13-12:24

The Christian Church is not an organization, but an organism, and if you, a member of it, live an un-christian life, you are injuring the whole Church of God. We shall be held responsible, not only for the evil which we have done, but also for the consequences of it in other lives; and we shall be held accountable also for all the good we might have done, and did not do.

Well may we pray with the psalmist:

'If Thou, LORD, shouldest mark iniquities, O Lord, who shall stand? But there is forgiveness with Thee, that Thou mayest be feared' (Psa. cxxx. 3, 4).

The Lord told Joshua that there would be no victory for Israel until sin in the camp had been searched out and judged; but when that was done He said:

'Fear not, neither be thou dismayed. Take all the people of war with thee, and arise, go up to Ai. See, I have given into thy hand the king of Ai, and his people, and his city, and his land' (ch. viii. 1).

There is a Jewish proverb that says:

'There are three men who get no pity—
an unsecured creditor, a hen-pecked husband,
and *a man that does not try again.*'

No Christian who has been overcome should sink into despondency, but rather should repent, and *try again*, more completely relying upon God. David and Peter and Mark all suffered defeat, but they all rose again to glorious victory. Failure in the past should teach us, and not paralyze us.

> Deem not the irrevocable past
>   As wholly wasted, wholly vain;
> For, rising on its wrecks, at last
>   To nobler greatness we attain.

There is a gospel of recoverability for all who will to live victoriously. Joshua again attacked Ai, this time taking *all* the men of war, and he completely destroyed it. His 'valley of Achor' became 'a door of hope' (Hos. ii. 15), and because his did, ours may. Let not past failure paralyze your present, or mortgage your future. Get right with God now, and *try again*.

Now, in the record of the central part of the great campaign in Canaan, there are two more incidents, so important both historically and spiritually, that we must call attention to them in our survey.

The first of these incidents relates to the proclamation of the Law at Mounts Ebal and Gerizim (ch. viii. 30-35); and the second relates to the deceiving of Joshua and the princes of Israel by the craftiness of the Gibeonites, which led to an alliance between them (ch. ix.).

The conjunction of these events is impressive and significant, occurring as they do in the midst of strenuous conflict; and it is noteworthy that the great pas-

sage in Eph. vi. 10-18, which addresses the Christian
soldier, has these words:

> 'Take the sword of the Spirit, which is the Word
> of God; praying always with all prayer and suppli-
> cation in the Spirit, and watching thereunto with all
> perseverance.'

Here the *Word of God* and *prayer* are shown to be
vitally related, and in the two passages in Joshua
which we are considering we see the Word of God
honoured at Shechem (ch. viii. 30-35), and prayer
neglected at Gilgal (ch. ix). But neither of these factors
is of any practical use without the other. A prayer-
less regard for the Word of God is of no avail, and
praying which neglects the Word of God is equally
unavailing.

After the proclamation of the law at Shechem, a
heathen tribe in the land came wilily to Joshua and
asked for a league with Israel. So genuine did their
appearance and story seem to be that 'Joshua made
peace with them, and made a league with them,
and *asked not counsel at the mouth of the LORD*' (ch. ix. 14, 15).
This alliance should never have been made, and would
never have been made if Joshua and the princes had
shown discretion as well as courage.

If we are subject to the Word of God we shall not
judge after the sight of the eyes, nor after the hearing
of the ears (Isa. xi. 3); we shall not be caught by the
wiles and devices of the devil.

It must have been noticed that Bible lectures are
much more popular than prayer-meetings, yet prayer
is a truer index to one's spiritual condition than is
Bible study. Prayer must be spiritual, but Bible
study may be largely, or even altogether, intellectual.

Beware of Gilgal after Shechem. Beware of the snares of everyday life after solemn avowals.

We have spoken of the central campaign in some detail because the historical record is detailed, occupying four chapters (vi—ix); and because alike in history and spiritual experience *beginnings* are of the utmost importance. A right start is a great asset in spiritual life, as well as in business, or in a race. It is in the beginnings of spiritual conflict that we have the opportunity to learn that we are very weak, and that God is very strong; to learn that self-confidence is folly, and that faith in God is wisdom; to learn that disobedience always brings disaster, and that obedience to the revealed will of God always ensures blessing; to learn that prayerlessness spells defeat, and that constant watchfulness, and humble reliance on the Almighty, must lead to victory. It will be well for us if we learn these lessons soon, for that will prevent many a sad experience later on in the fight.

After the conquest of central Canaan Joshua turned his attention, first to the south, and then to the north; and, as we have said, the fate of the south depended upon two battles, at Gibeon, and at Beth-horon; and the fate of the north, upon one battle, at the waters of Merom. In neither of these two campaigns were the mistakes repeated which had been made in the first campaign. Here there was no self-confidence, no disobedience, no covetousness, and no prayerlessness; but, on the contrary, simple faith in God, prompt action, and uncompromising warfare.

For new situations new methods were employed; there was an adaptation of means to ends; hearts were brave, minds were alert, and hands were busy. It was

so then, and it must be so now, if we would win our
battles, if we would conquer all our foes.

Many are the lessons we may learn from this second
part of the Book of Joshua, which tells of the Christian
conflict.   We should learn:

   that as long as sin lasts, conflict with it will be
      necessary:

   that in the conflict the alternatives are victory or
      defeat:

   that in this fight with evil we have a divine
      Captain, to follow whom obediently and
      courageously makes us more than con-
      querors:

   that no evil is so insignificant as to allow of partial
      measures in dealing with it:

   that when we are defeated, the cause may be
      discovered by prayer, but

   that it will take more than prayer to repair the
      damage:

   that the work of subduing our enemies is not
      sudden, but gradual:

   that success in one battle does not win the cam-
      paign, and defeat in one battle does not
      mean that the whole campaign has been lost:

   that divine help and human exertion must go
      together; that God uses our efforts to fulfil
      His ends, and fights for them who fight for
      Him:

   that as the enemies of God are manifold, the
      method of dealing with them must be multi-
      form:

   that trusting and trying are not contradictory,
      but complementary:

JOSHUA 5:13-12:24

that the Law of God is given, not for our admiration, but for our obedience; the Law in which there is an Ebal as well as a Gerizim:

that when extermination of foes is commanded, confederation with them is a sin:

that we should keep a record of spiritual victories for the glory of God, for our own encouragement, and for the instruction of others.

THE REVIEW OF THE CONQUEST (Ch. 12)

This last lesson is taught in ch. xii of Joshua, which ends the second division of the Book. The *precision* and *completeness* of this review of the conquests are noteworthy. Here is no general statement of victory, but one detailed and circumstantial, for particular blessings deserve something more than general recognition. Joshua first details the victories on the east of the Jordan (2-6); then, on the west of the River (7-24); which were, first, in the centre of the land; then, in the south; then, in the north; and, finally, the number of conquered kings is stated to be thirty-one (24).

It will be well for us if at the end of life's day we have such recollections as these; if, like Paul, we can say:

'I have fought a good fight; I have finished the course; I have kept the faith.'

Such testimony will not be in a spirit of pharisaical boasting, but in gratitude to Him who called us to the conflict, and enabled us to conquer. Those of us whose battles lie now for the most part in the past, may well remember to emulate Goldsmith's broken soldier in *The Deserted Village*, who

> Wept o'er his wounds, or, tales of sorrow done,
> Shoulder'd his crutch, and show'd how fields were won.

And you, whose battles for the most part lie yet before you, learn from the doughty warriors who have preceded you; profit by their failures, follow their faith, repeat their victories, realize their ideals, and at last with red sword, dented helmet, and many a scar, it may be, you will have a share in that shout which will bring the foes of every Jericho crashing to their doom.

> Stand then in His great might,
>   With all His strength endued;
> And take, to arm you for the fight,
>   The panoply of God;
> That, having all things done,
>   And all your conflicts passed,
> Ye may o'ercome through Christ alone,
>   And stand complete at last.

JOSHUA 5:13-12:24

3

POSSESSING THE LAND

Joshua 13-24

IN our survey we have considered *Entering the Land* and *Conquering the Land;* but the story is not yet complete. A third division, which comprises half the Book, tells of *Possessing the Land.*

It cannot be claimed that this division makes easy reading, for there are hundreds of names of persons and places, and for the latter to be intelligible a map of Canaan must be before the reader all the time.

But let it not be thought that this part of the book is only, or chiefly, of historical and geographical interest. No part of Holy Scripture is that, but here the persons and places derive their main significance from the moral and spiritual teaching which they present.

We have called attention several times to the historical and spiritual connection between the divisions of this book. The Land had first to be *entered,* and then *conquered,* before it could be *possessed;* and, in like manner, the *life* which the *land* anticipates, must be *entered* upon, and maintained by faith and effort, by *conflict* and conquest, before it can be a life of growingly rich *possession* of those blessings which are ours 'in the heavenlies in Christ Jesus' (Eph. i. 3).

And attention must again be called to the distinction, historically and spiritually, between the *inheritance* and the *possession* (Deut. xix. 2, 3, 14).

Historically, the *inheritance* is the whole geographical

area which God gave to Israel, 'from the river of Egypt, unto the great river, the river Euphrates' (Gen. xv. 18), which, however, they never possessed; and the *possession* is that much only of the inheritance which they did take.

And spiritually, the *inheritance* is all that God has given to His people in Christ, everything that He could give, that is, Christ Himself; and the *possession* is that much of Christ which every believer, and the whole Church, appropriate; and, needless to say, no one has ever possessed as much of Christ as he might and should have done.

This distinction, then, makes the study of this third division of our subject of the utmost importance; for, from the Book of Joshua we may learn what are the *principles of possessing,* the *preventives of possession,* and the *perils of the possessor.*

But before looking at this in detail, let us observe how this third division of the book is introduced (Ch. 13:1-6).

> 'Now Joshua was old and stricken in years; and the LORD said unto him: "Thou art old and stricken in years, and *there remaineth yet very much land to be possessed. This is the land that yet remaineth* (1, 2).
>
> "All the inhabitants will I drive out from before the children of Israel; only divide thou it by lot unto the Israelites for an inheritance, as I have commanded thee"' (6).

Six chapters have told us of the conflicts and conquests of the people (vi—xi), which must have taken about seven years (xi. 18), and yet, after all that, *there remained very much land to be possessed,* and *many enemies to be driven out.*

The lessons here are manifold and rich. This situation should teach the Christian that there is no completeness of experience here on earth, that there is no present perfection, but that all the time, and all the way, we may have the vision of unattained possibilities. However old we are, and however far we have gone in appropriating what is ours, it is still true that

> ' there remaineth yet very much land to be possessed.'

'Keswick' never did teach, and never could teach sinless perfection. Such an idea, in the light of the facts, would itself be sin. Jesus said what no one else has ever been able to say truthfully, 'I have finished the work which Thou gavest Me to do' (John xvii. 4). At its end the life of each of us will be unfinished, as so often a broken column over a grave implies.

We do not win all the battles we fight, and we do not fight all the battles which there are to be fought. This is not a depressing but an inspiring fact and truth. If at any stage of life we could believe that we had exhausted the possibilities of life, we would at once become the most miserable creatures alive, for we live, not in accomplishment, but in hope. Paul's language must be ours:

> 'Not that I have already obtained, or am already made perfect; but I press on, if so be that I may apprehend that for which also I was apprehended by Christ Jesus.
>
> 'I count not myself yet to have apprehended; but one thing I do; forgetting the things which are behind, and stretching forward to the things which are before, I press on toward the goal, unto the prize of the high calling of God in Christ Jesus' (Phil. iii. 12-14).

It would be a sad thing to think of life ending with work not done, if accomplishment was bounded by earth and time; but it is not.

Faith will claim the unwon, and as we may complete what those who went before us began, so those who follow us will be expected to complete what we have begun. Conflict will never cease while enemies remain, and so new conquests are always possible.

> 'A man's reach should exceed his grasp, or what's a heaven for?'

Now let us consider

SOME PRINCIPLES OF POSSESSING

By this is meant the means whereby one possesses little or much of what there is to be possessed. Remarks scattered here and there throughout this part of the record throw much light on this matter. Let us look at a few of these.

First, we are told that *possession is by conflict* (Ch. 17:14-18).

This conflict differs from that of chs. vi—xi, in that while *it* was the work of the whole army, *this* refers to the military energies of two tribes, 'the children of Joseph', Ephraim and Manasseh. The distinction is between corporate and individual conflict. This passage (Ch. 17:14-18) is full of lessons of the first importance. The facts from which the lessons emerge are:

first, the children of Joseph claimed to be 'a great people', and complained that their portion of the inheritance was not commensurate with their importance (14):

second, Joshua told them that if they wanted
more room, they should, by energetic effort,
take it from their enemies (15):

third, the children of Joseph replied that their
enemies had 'chariots of iron', and were
numerous (18):

fourth, Joshua answered that if they wanted the
territory they must win it by driving out their
foes, chariots notwithstanding (17, 18).

From this chapter (vers. 12, 13), and a later record
(Judg. i. 27-29), we learn that the children of Joseph
did not drive out their enemies, but put them to
tribute.

Now remember that these are people who had
crossed the Jordan, and had shared in the conquest
of Canaan; but here a bright spotlight is turned on
them, separating them from the nation as such, and
revealing them in their individuality.

From these particulars it will not be difficult for us
to see, if we want to, the application of this incident
to ourselves.

Our individual character cannot rightly be discerned
and appraised while we are viewed only as a member
of the Christian Church, of a community of people.
True judgment begins at close quarters, and it is when
the divine spotlight is turned upon the individual that
he may lose the halo which his associations may have
given him.

The children of Joseph were numerous, they were
the people of which Joshua came, they aspired to
predominance over the other tribes, and they were
proud. It was this which led them to think of themselves as 'a great people', and to complain that their

portion was 'too narrow', was 'not enough', for them.

Is there nothing of this spirit in Christians to-day? Do we not need to be reminded constantly that in the Church God is no respecter of persons? He will give no one more consideration than others because he belongs to a good family, or because he is well educated, or because he belongs to the professional class, or because he is a member of the State Church, or because he belongs to the Brethren, the Methodists, or the Baptists! These labels do not secure preference or preferment in the spiritual realm; and greatness does not consist in the accidental and incidental in life, but in the individual's entire reliance upon God, faithful adherence to duty, and courageous enterprise in the pursuit of practical holiness. God's promises are conditioned, and the conditions must be fulfilled if the promises are to be enjoyed.

Let us not, like the children of Joseph, fail to drive out our enemies because we prefer ease to exertion, and compromise to conflict. Let us not worry about our dignity, but rather determine to do our duty. Great claims should be matched by great achievements. He who would have, must dare and do in the Name of the Lord his God.

Secondly, we see that *possession is by providence* (Ch. 13:6).

In this third division of the Book of Joshua the word 'lot' occurs twenty-five times, beginning in ch. xiii. 6. In Israel of old it was a divinely-appointed means of learning what the will of the Lord was.

> 'The lot is cast into the lap; but the whole disposing thereof is of the LORD' (Prov. xvi. 33).

JOSHUA 13-24

The Rabbis have spent much ingenuity in speculating how the 'lot' was taken, but what mattered was the meaning, not the method, and the meaning was that by this method God was giving to each of the tribes that place and portion in and of the land which His wisdom intended for them.   To believe that this was so, is to invest these chapters with quite a new significance and interest.

In our time, in place of the 'lot' are the Holy Spirit, the Word of God, the Throne of Grace, and the open or closed door, that is, circumstances.   By these means we may discover what God's will for us is, and if we are subject to them, these means will never fail us.

No one who believes this can believe in *chance,* or *luck,* but he will believe that 'all things work together for good to them that love God' (Rom. viii. 28).   One's belief determines his attitude towards all things, and if a Christian does not believe in a divine unerring and loving Providence, who guides in all the minor, as in all the major affairs of life, he cannot, as he should, possess his inheritance in Christ.

The difference made by believing and not believing this truth is illustrated by the history of Abraham, and of Lot.   Abraham believed in providence, and let God choose for him, but Lot chose for himself, and came to disaster.   The one walked by faith and the other by sight, and we see now to what goals those paths led.

Are you letting God choose your lot in the inheritance, or are you making a plan of life for yourself, choosing your own path, determining your own career, and trusting to your own wit and wisdom for guidance?

Listen to these words of Horace Bushnell:

> 'God has a definite life-plan for every human person, girding him, visibly or invisibly, for some exact thing, which it will be the true significance and glory of his life to have accomplished.

> 'Oh, to live out such a life as God appoints, how great a thing it is—to do the duties, make the sacrifices, bear the adversities, finish the plan, and then to say with Christ (who of us will be able?), "It is finished."'

Thirdly, we learn that *possession is by request* (Ch. 15:16-19)

Here is a simple and beautiful story. Caleb promised to give his daughter as wife to the man who would attack and take Kirjath-sepher, 'the city of books.' Caleb's nephew Othniel did this; Achsah became his wife; and Caleb gave to her as a possession the southland or Negeb, which was an arid region. Achsah was not satisfied with this, and during the marriage celebrations she approached her father Caleb who asked her, 'What do you want?' and this was her reply:

> 'Give me a blessing; for you have given me a south land, give me also springs of water'.

> 'And he gave her the upper springs and the nether springs'.

For our present purpose the important words in this passage are:

> ' You have given me; give me also; and he gave her.'

These words we may take over into the New Testament, and apply them to Christ and ourselves. Every

JOSHUA 13-24

believer can say to Him, '*Thou hast given me*', and we
may well contemplate what He has given us; but could
we know all that we have received from Him, we may
still say, '*give me also*'.   Having any portion in Christ
should lead us to long for more.   So far as possession
of our inheritance is concerned, no true Christian can
ever feel satisfied, but will ever be yearning for and
reaching forth towards something more, a richer
portion, a completer blessing.

> Jesus, grace for grace outpouring,
>   Show me ever greater things;
> Raise me higher, sunward soaring,
>   Mounting as on eagle-wings.
> By the brightness of Thy face,
> Jesus, let me grow in grace.
>
> Let me, then, be always growing,
>   Never, never standing still,
> Listening, learning, better knowing
>   Thee, and Thy most blessed will.

If we will but say to Him: '*Thou hast given me: give
me also*', how swift He will be to bestow blessings more
and richer.   He will give to us 'upper and nether
springs', so that we shall be like a well-watered garden.
The Lord's liberality only awaits our longing.   If we
thirst for springs of heavenly life, we shall find that
they are flowing just where we are; we shall realize
that 'He satisfieth the longing soul, and filleth the
hungry soul with goodness'.

> '*Thou hast given me; give me also; and he gave*'.
> 'Ask, and it shall be given unto you;
>   seek, and ye shall find;
>   knock, and it shall be opened unto you' (Matt. vii. 7).
> 'Ye have not, because ye ask not' (Jas. iv. 2).

'What things soever ye desire, when ye pray, believe that ye have received them, and ye shall have
them' (Mk. xi. 24).

'No good thing will He withhold from them that
walk uprightly' (Ps. lxxxiv. 11).

Fourthly, it is shown that *possession is by capacity*
(Ch. 17:16; 19:9,47).

Three brief expressions in the narrative raise and
illumine this subject. They are, *not enough*, in ch. xvii.
16; *too much*, in ch. xix. 9; and *too little*, in ch. xix. 47.
In the first passage the children of Joseph said that the
portion which had been given to them was *not enough*, and
they claimed more, but were not prepared to fight for
it (ch. xvii. 14-18). In the second passage it is said that
the portion of Judah was *too much* for them, and so the
children of Simeon had their inheritance within the
border of Judah's portion. In the third passage it is
stated that 'the coast of the children of Dan went out
too little for them', and so they fought, conquered, and
possessed more.

That is all that need be said on the historical aspect
of the subject, but these expressions suggest the whole
subject of spiritual capacity, by which is meant, *receiving and holding power*. Think of that for a moment:
receiving and holding power!

Each of us has this power in measure, but the measure
greatly differs in individuals. The capacity of some
is large, and of others, small, but no Christian is without ability, in some degree, to receive and hold things
that are spiritual; indeed, without this ability one could
not be a Christian at all.

Now, in these talks, we have been regarding the
believer's inheritance to be Christ Himself, 'in whom

dwelleth all the fulness of the Deity bodily, and in whom we come to fulness of life' (Col. ii. 9, 10). Therefore by *capacity* we mean the ability to apprehend and appropriate Christ, who is the redeeming revelation of God.

This ability in believers differs, not only in degree, but also in substance. My meaning can be made clear, perhaps, by an illustration.

A lady missionary and I were talking about the Lord, and in course of conversation she said: 'Mr. Scroggie, I have a Christ you have not got'. I was somewhat taken aback, and asked her what she meant, and she replied, in effect:

'Just because I am what I am, a compound of certain abilities, the product of my upbringing and outlook, with the mental, moral, and emotional constitution which is *mine*—just because of all this, I have needs which no one else has, as there is not a second of me; and as Christ alone meets these needs, I have a Christ which no one else can have'.

I saw the point at once, and my thought went to the passage in Eph. iii. 18, 19:

'That you may be able to apprehend, *with all the saints*, what is the breadth, and length, and height, and depth, and to know the love of Christ which passeth knowledge, that you may be filled unto all the fulness of God.'

I take that to mean, not that any one saint can grasp all that is there set forth of Christ, but that one will grasp this, and another, that, and that all the saints will be needed to grasp the five dimensions of Christ. This is what is meant by *capacity*, as I am now speaking of it; *possession of our inheritance in Christ is by capacity.* Each of us can have as much of Christ as he is capable of having; and must we not all admit that we have never possessed that much of Him; but if we are conscious to-day that we have *not enough,* that we have *too little,* then, like the children of Dan, we shall resolve, whatever the cost, to have more of Him.

Another word before we pass from this. *Capacity* is not something rigid, like an iron box, but something supple and elastic; it is a faculty that becomes larger with use. The more anyone has of Christ, the more he is capable of having. If we grasp all of Him that is within our reach to-day, there will be more of Him for us to grasp to-morrow; and we shall never be able to say, as did the children of Judah, that our portion is *too much.*

Fifthly, it is clear that *possession is also by faith* (Ch. 14).

In this record a whole chapter is given to Caleb, and an instructive chapter it is. Here an old man, aged eighty-five (10) goes back in memory forty-five years to the time when he and Joshua and ten others were sent into Canaan to spy out the land. On their return, ten of the twelve spies urged against Israel's entrance into the land, because of the giants there; and the other two, Joshua and Caleb, urged that the people should go in, because they believed that the Lord would give them victory over the Canaanites. The ten had big giants and a little God, and the two had a big God and little giants.

For Caleb's part in this crisis, forty-five years before,

the Lord promised to him for a possession, part of the land in which he had spied. Since then, forty-five years had passed, and now Caleb claims the fulfilment of the promise. He says: 'Now therefore give me this mountain, whereof the LORD spake in that day. ... And Joshua blessed Caleb, and gave unto him Hebron for an inheritance' (12, 13).

For forty-five years this man's life had been built on a promise which God had given to him. He believed the promise, and waited patiently for its fulfilment, and when the hour came, he put in his claim, and God honoured it.

Now the Bible is full of promises, which are called 'precious and exceeding great' (2 Pet. i. 4), and it is the duty, as well as the privilege, of Christians to *believe* them. Evan Hopkins used to speak of having *a good believing time*, and it is when we do that, that we add to our possession of the inheritance which is already ours.

God is faithful Who has promised, but if we are unbelieving all that He would do for us remains undone. Jesus said that He could not do His mighty works in certain places because of their unbelief. *Unbelief* is not *disbelief*. The difference between these is the same as the difference between *neglecting* and *rejecting*, or between saying *nothing* and saying *no*.

We would find it a humbling if not a shattering experience, to go through the promises of the Bible, and of each one to ask ourselves—*do I believe this?*

'My grace is sufficient for thee'. 'Ask and it shall be given unto you; seek and ye shall find; knock and it shall be opened unto you'. 'God will not suffer you to be tempted above that ye are able, but will with

the temptation also make a way to escape, that ye may
be able to bear it'. 'I will guide thee with mine eye
upon thee'. 'When thou passest through the waters
I will be with thee'. 'I have blotted out as a thick
cloud thy transgressions'. 'My peace I give unto
you'. 'I am with thee; I will strengthen thee; I will
help thee; I will uphold thee'. 'I will heal your
backsliding.' 'Those that seek me early shall find
me'. 'I will give unto you power over all the power
of the enemy'.

Do we believe these promises with the faith that
affects our conduct? So many of them are not
believed because they are conditioned, and too
often we are unwilling to obey the precepts on which
the promises are based. Well, what is crystal clear
is that, if we would possess more of our divine Inheritance we must obediently believe God's promises.

> Only believe; only believe.
> All things are possible,
> Only believe.

Here, then, are five ways in which we may, more
and more, possess our inheritance: by *conflict;* by
providence; by *request;* by *capacity;* and by *faith.* These
are some of the means whereby we may traverse the
Land which is Life, and enjoy that rest which is un-
tiring energy and activity.

How is it, then, that notwithstanding all this promise
and prospect, we are so spiritually poor and weak?

This leads us now to the consideration, all too
briefly, I fear, of

SOME PREVENTIVES OF POSSESSION.

Of these, we have time to mention three only, but

JOSHUA 13-24

they are largely representative and comprehensive.

First of all there is *slackness* (Ch. 18:3).

> 'Joshua said unto the children of Israel,
>> "How long are ye *slack* to go to possess the land
>>> which the Lord God of your fathers hath
>>> given you?"'

'Slack' is a word full of corrupt ingredients. It is used in the Old Testament in at least three senses, closely related to one another, and each of the three helps us to see the sin of the Israelites in the passage before us.

First of all, to be *slack* means to be *slothful, idle, lazy, indolent,* and the word is so used in Prov. x. 4; xii. 24; xix. 15. With this sin the Israelites were chargeable. After their many conflicts in the land they became disposed to indulge in a season of respite, and to rest satisfied with what they had gained, and hence Joshua's remonstrance.

Now this is a very dangerous state of heart and mind for a Christian to be in, and should be regarded, not as weakness, but as sin. To slacken our interest and energy in spiritual advancement is to grieve the Holy Spirit, to rob ourselves of blessing, to hinder other people, and to encourage the enemy. No Christian will win a race who stops to take a breather; nor will he win a fight, who asks for compassionate leave.

Secondly, to be *slack* means to *fail*, to *fall short* of an appointed end, to be found *wanting;* and in this sense it is used in Josh. i. 5, where the Lord tells Joshua that He will not *fail* him.

This is another word which should fill us with fear, for in ends that are true and worthy it is a terrible thing to *fail*. In Christ we have a magnificent opportunity and a marvellous prospect, and to *fall short* of it,

to be *found wanting* in the day of testing, is one of the
saddest of experiences. To have a prize within one's
reach and yet not to grasp it; to be within sight of a
goal and yet not to get to it; almost to win a victory
and yet to lose it—this indeed is tragic; yet does it not
describe the case of many?

Thirdly, to be *slack* means to *delay,* to *tarry,* to *defer,*
to *put off,* and the word is so used in such passages as
Exod. xxii. 29; Deut. xxiii. 21; Prov. xxiii. 30; Eccles.
v. 4; Hab. ii. 3.

This differs somewhat from the other meanings in
that it implies good intention; but good intentions are
of no use unless they are translated into good actions.
To *intend* is not to *do,* and while we are intending we
may lose the opportunity of doing. To be thus slack
is perilous and sinful where Christ is the Prize.

Well may it be asked to-day, as it was long ago,

> 'How long are ye slack to go to possess the land,
>   which the LORD God of your fathers hath given you?'

> Let not your hands be slack,
>   Grip thou thy sword!
> Why should'st thou courage lack?
>   Think of thy Lord.
> Did He not fight for thee?
> Stronger than all is He,
> And He thy strength will be,
>   Rest on His word.

> Let not thy hands be slack,
>   Haste to the fray!
> Dream not of turning back;
>   Life is not play!
> Gird thou thy armour on,
> Fight till the battle's won,
> Then shall thy Lord's 'Well done',
>   More than repay.

JOSHUA 13-24

Another preventive of possession is *compromise* (Ch. 16:10)

> Ephraim 'drave not out the Canaanites, but the Canaanites dwelt in the midst of Ephraim, and became servants to do task work'.

Ephraim could have driven out the Canaanites, but they did not choose to do so. They found it an easier task to let the enemy remain in their midst, and to make what use they could of them for profit. But that was not what God had told them to do, and such action is known as *compromise*.

Perhaps it is not an exaggeration to say that this is the besetting sin of Christians. Compromise is the endeavour to make the best of incompatibles, and this is fatal alike in the regenerate person, and in the Christian Church. The devil's attack upon Jesus in the wilderness was an attempt to get Him to compromise His *faith*, in the matter of the bread; His *reason*, in the matter of falling from the pinnacle of the temple; and His *conscience*, in the matter of who He should worship; and Jesus hurled back the temptation at every point.

These are still the cardinal points of compromise. Every Christian who is compromising is doing so, either by withdrawing from simple faith in God, or by abandoning his commonsense for popularity, or by violating his conscience for temporary gain, and such compromise is always fatal.

The church that sets out to spiritualize the world, will soon find that the world will secularize the church. When wheat and tares compromise, it is the wheat that suffers. Light and darkness, right and wrong, good and evil, truth and error are incompatibles,

and when they compromise it is the light, the right,
the good, and the truth that are damaged.

Have nothing to do with compromise where principle is concerned.

And yet another preventive of possession is *inability*.

In ch. xv. 63, we read that Judah *could not drive out* the Jebusites; and in ch. xvii. 12, that Manasseh *could not drive out* the Canaanites. Why could they not drive them out, seeing that it was God's will that they should? This is a humiliating admission of failure, and the reasons for it must be found in themselves, in a want of faith, of vision, of hope, and therefore of power.

It is not the will of God that any sin should be resident in a believer's life, that any evil should remain unsubdued; yet are there not such sins and evils in us? And when we are told what to do with them, do we say, 'I cannot'?

If that be the case of anyone here, let him or her consider what is implied by that conclusion. The real question is not, *can we?* but 'can God?' Of course *we cannot,* and it is folly ever to have thought that we could be a match for our enemies; but when all the resources of the Almighty are at our disposal, it is not only foolishness, but wickedness to give up and admit defeat. Rather should our language be, 'I can do all things in Him that strengtheneth me' (Phil. iv. 13).

> Against me earth and hell combine;
> But on my side is power divine;
> Jesus is all, and He is mine.

We have considered *Some Principles of Possessing,* and

Some Preventives of Possession, and now to conclude, let us contemplate

SOME PERILS OF THE POSSESSOR

We have nearly completed our survey of the Book of Joshua in its three divisions of *Entering, Conquering,* and *Possessing* the Land, but one or two matters of much importance remain for our consideration; and these relate, let us remember, to a people who have gone far in the fulfilment of God's purpose for them. The conquest and allotment of the land did not mean the end of difficulties and dangers for the Israelites, for they still had enemies without, and evils within.

And this is true also of that which this whole story adumbrates. There is no stage of spiritual advancement at which we are delivered from sinful attack and temptation, from weaknesses which expose us to danger, and from the perils of ignorance and indolence; and so a time never comes during our earthly life when we no longer stand in need of the merits of Christ's sacrifice, of the aid of the Holy Spirit, of earnest prayerfulness and constant watchfulness, and of the provision which God has made for our ignorance and human frailty.

Let us briefly consider three perils which confront believers who have entered into the experience of spiritual rest.

And first, *the peril of misunderstanding* (Ch. 22).

This is the classic chapter in the Bible on misunderstandings among God's people, and the story can be briefly told.

The two tribes of Reuben and Gad, and half the tribe of Manasseh, had asked to have their possession on the east of Jordan, and this was agreed to, on the condition that their men of war should go into Canaan with the other tribes, and fight with them until the land was conquered. This they did; and with Joshua's gratitude and blessing they returned to their territory on the east of the River. When they reached the Jordan they built an altar of witness, an altar which would speak to following generations of their religious and national oneness with Israel.

JOSHUA 13-24

The tribes in the land, whom they had so recently left, heard about this structure, and concluded that it was an altar of sacrifice, making evident religious schism and tribal secession on the part of the two and a half tribes; and the army of Israel prepared to go to war with them.

But before actually doing so, a priest and ten princes were sent to the two and a half tribes to make enquiry. They charged them with rebellion against the Lord, and disloyalty to Israel, and warned them of the grave consequences.

The two and a half tribes were astonished at the construction that had been put upon their innocent act and worthy motives, and had no difficulty in convincing the deputation that their interpretation of the matter was utterly wrong. It is well that the affair was cleared up, for had war eventuated, the very existence of Israel would have been threatened.

But, it may be asked, what has this to do with us? A great deal, I suspect; for among Christians perhaps there is nothing more grievous and damaging than misunderstandings. They so easily arise; they so swiftly spread; and the further they go the worse they get.

I venture to say that if all misunderstandings existing at present among Christians were cleared up, the Christian Church would be in a state of revival.

Why is it that we are so ready to listen to gossip that is damaging to others? Why is it that we are so quick to impute motives for the actions of our fellows? Why is it that we are so disposed to put the ugliest interpretation on what other people say and do? Why is it that we are so willing to draw unfavourable inferences from mere rumours? Can what was said of the Prince Consort be said of us?

> He spake no slander;
> No, nor listened to it.

It would have been well if the priest and princes had made inquiries before they had drawn their conclusion; and it will be well if we do the same. It will be in vain for us to sing hymns, and go into raptures over addresses, if we have made no attempt to end estrangements with our fellow believers in the family, in business, and in the church. Are there people at home, or abroad, who are heavy of spirit, or broken of heart, because of your unjust treatment of them, because of your false judgments on their justifiable actions? They are not singing, as you are:

> 'Oh, blissful self-surrender, to live, my Lord, by Thee'.
> 'My whole is on the altar, I'm waiting for the fire'.
> 'Have Thine own way, Lord, have Thine own way'.

No, they are not singing, but suffering, and if you would have them sing, you must clear up those misunderstandings which have so impeded *your* spiritual progress, if not theirs, which have chilled the hearts of not a few, and which are a blot upon Christian profession.

In the second place there is *the peril of blunder* (Ch. 20:1-9).

Chapter xx of Joshua tells us that six *Cities of Refuge* were provided for the Israelites, three on the east, and three on the west of the Jordan, and it tells us *why* they were provided. They were to be shelters for anyone who had unintentionally killed another person.

What is given here briefly is set forth at greater length in Num. xxxv. 9-34, and Deut. xix. 1-13. In all these passages an idea occurs repeatedly to which we now call attention. It is found in the words *unawares, ignorantly,* and *unwittingly*. If a man had killed another without intending to do so, he had to flee to a City of Refuge, if he would save his own life. His case was then tried by Levites, and if it was found that the deed was an accident, the doer of it had to remain in the City of Refuge until the death of the high priest who was then in office, and after that, he could return home.

Now these passages bring before us the fact that we may sin without intending to do so, but, we are told, what is done is sin nevertheless.

Here is a whole area of experience that we may well explore; and this is a matter we must not omit from our prayers. What is contrary to the perfect righteousness and holiness of God is sin; and we all must be constantly thinking, saying, and doing things unwittingly which are sin in His sight. Such things may be due to carelessness, to misunderstanding, to haste, or to other causes, but they are wrong, and must be dealt with. It was not enough for the man who had slain another to say that he had not intended to do so, for he had in fact done so, and the event had to be judged.

The provision for that man was the City of Refuge; but the provision for us is Christ, to whom we flee for refuge to lay hold on the hope set before us. Day by day we need to claim His atoning merits for our unintentional errors, for our inadvertent mistakes, for the suffering and sorrow which we have unwittingly inflicted on other people, and for our blundering goodness.

Finally, there is *the peril of apostasy* (Ch. 23:12).

Joshua pointed out to the Israelites a terrible possibility when he said, 'if ye do in any wise *go back*.' Of such an act a psalmist uses the word *turn aside* (cxxv. 5); Isaiah says, *gone away backward* (i. 4); Zephaniah says, *turned back* (i. 6); the writer to the Hebrews says, *draw back* (x. 39); and Peter speaks of this sad experience as *being again entangled and overcome,* and as *turning from* the way of righteousness (2 Peter ii. 20, 21); from which passages we see that the dark and dread shadow of apostasy falls over the whole landscape of religious profession.

There is no level of Christian experience from which we may not *go back;* we may turn our back on all the light we have ever received; we may 'count the blood of the covenant wherewith we were sanctified an unholy thing, and do despite unto the Spirit of grace' (Heb. x. 29); we may throw away the gathered spiritual experiences of a lifetime, and forfeit a reward which had been gained. Apostasy is the abandonment of beliefs or principles which were once professed.

These perils confront the Christian all along the way, but instead of paralyzing us with fear, they should lead us to discover our resources of protection and provision in our risen Lord, and to find in Him the secret of holy rest in a conscience void of offence.

Let us, then, 'possess our possessions', and not, as some of old, 'be still, and take them not' (Obad. 17; 1 Kings xxii. 3).

JOSHUA 13-24

> O blessed life, heart, mind, and soul,
>   From self-born aims and wishes free,
>   In all at one with Deity,
> And loyal to the Lord's control.
>
> O life, how blessed, how divine,
>   High life, the earnest of a higher;
>   Saviour, fulfil my deep desire,
> And let this blessed life be mine.

4

LIFE MORE ABUNDANT

WE have endeavoured to show how momentous for Israel, and indeed for the whole world, were those first twenty-five years of the nation in Canaan, under the leadership of Joshua.

As history the period is vital and crucial, but it is a great deal more than history, for the New Testament affirms that the experiences of the Israelites were typical and prophetical of things to come. The Apostle Paul says, 'In these things they became figures of us'; and again, 'these things happened unto them by way of figure, and they were written for our admonition' (1 Cor. x. 6, 11).

The land into which Israel entered tells of another sphere of life, and the rest into which they entered there, tells of a richer quality of life than they could possibly know.

Embedded and embodied in the historical facts of the Book are the spiritual truths, and it is these latter that are of significance for us.

And now, leaving the historical 'figures', let us think only of that which is prefigured; and in doing so, we shall follow three leading thoughts, *Revelation, Experience,* and *Service*.

First of all, then,

REVELATION

No one can read the New Testament with any degree of insight and understanding without being impressed by the high level on which its thought moves when dealing with the subject of the Christian life. This is especially noticeable in the Writings of the Apostle Paul, in which phrase after phrase stands out in mystic grandeur of truths which have their origin in heaven, and their home in the heart.

Here are a few examples:

'To me to live is Christ' (Phil. i. 21).

'I count all things to be loss for the excellency of the knowledge of Christ Jesus my Lord'

'I count all things . . . but refuse that I may gain Christ' (Phil. iii. 8).

'I have been crucified with Christ; and it is no longer I that live, but Christ liveth in me; and that life which I now live in the flesh I live in faith, the faith which is in the Son of God, who loved me, and gave Himself up for me' (Gal. ii. 20).

'Through the cross of our Lord Jesus Christ, the world has been crucified unto me, and I unto the world' (Gal. vi. 14).

'We may walk in newness of life'.

'Reckon ye yourselves to be dead unto sin, but alive unto God in Christ Jesus'.

'Sin shall not have dominion over you'.

'Made free from sin, ye have your fruit unto sanctification' (Rom. vi. 4, 11, 14, 22).

'The fruit of the Spirit is love, joy, peace, long-suffering, kindness, goodness, faithfulness, meekness, self-control' (Gal. vi. 23).

'The word of God abideth in you, and ye have overcome the evil one' (1 John ii. 14):

and the words of our Lord,

'I came that they may have life, and may have it abundantly' (John x. 10).

Accompanying such passages as these are others which point the way to the realization of the blessed secret:

> 'Leaving the word of the beginning of Christ, let us press on unto full growth' (Heb. vi. 1).
>
> 'He who began a good work in you will perfect it until the day of Jesus Christ' (Phil. i. 6).
>
> 'Be filled with the Spirit' (Eph. v. 18).
>
> 'Filled unto all the fulness of God' (Eph. iii. 19).
>
> 'In Him you have come to fulness of life' (Col. ii. 10).
>
> 'Having therefore these promises, . . . let us cleanse ourselves from all defilement of flesh and spirit, perfecting holiness in the fear of God' (2 Cor. vii. 1).

But there is another class of passages which shows the want and need of the blessings just referred to; passages which illustrate the sad fact that one may have *life,* and yet not have it *abundantly;* that one may be assured of spiritual *union* with Christ, and yet be a stranger to that *communion* with Him which is the outcome alone of trust and obedience.

Paul, remonstrating with the fickle Galatians, said,

> 'Are ye so foolish? Having begun in the Spirit, are ye now perfected in the flesh?' (Gal. iii. 3).

Better instructed Christians than they were are making the same mistake, and the matter is of vital importance, for we can never rise to the level of experience set forth in the former passages so long as we are providing substitutes for the Holy Spirit.

But there is another passage of profound significance in this connection, which you will find in Rom. vii. 15-24. I will read it from the Revised Standard Version:

> I do not do what I want, but I do the very thing I hate. Now if I do what I do not want, I agree that the law is good. So then it is no longer I that do it, but sin which dwells within me. For I know that nothing good dwells within me, that is, in my flesh. I can will what is right, but I cannot do it.

> For I do not do the good I want, but the evil I do not want is what I do. Now if I do what I do not want, it is no longer I that do it, but sin which dwells within me.

> So I find it to be a law that when I want to do right, evil lies close at hand. For I delight in the law of God, in my inmost self, but I see in my members another law at war with the law of my mind and making me captive to the law of sin which dwells in my members. Wretched man that I am! Who will deliver me from this body of death?'

Some regard this passage to be a description of an unregenerate man struggling to keep the law; and others regard it to be a description of a regenerate man trying in the energy of the flesh to live a true Christian life. To debate this matter is not within the scope of our present purpose, but I will say two things about it: *firstly*, that the cry here is not for deliverance from sin's *guilt*, but from its *power;* it is not for forgiveness of sins, but for help against indwelling sin; it concerns, not a state of condemnation, but a state of bondage; and *secondly*, that the experience here described is that of very many Christians, though it is far removed from Christian experience.

The message of holiness relates not so much to pardon as to power; not so much to guilt as to liberty. We have said and seen that for the conquest of our enemies there must be vigorous effort, but the struggle here described is not with anything without, but of ourselves within, of self with law.

These and other passages reveal the need of the blessings which are the heritage of the people of God, and from such Scriptures we must conclude that Christians generally have been, and are, content with an experience far removed from the divine ideal. We have made the intellectual apprehension of truth a substitute for the power of it in our own hearts, and we are in danger of regarding Christianity as a *philosophy*, rather than as a *life*.

Bishop Lightfoot has well said that

> 'Faith in Christ is a moral as well as an intellectual state, and with St. Paul its moral aspect is in fact the more prominent of the two'.

And he has shown that

> 'Christ contains the complete answer to the errors alike of Judaism and Hellenism; to the false ground of hope in the one, and to the false theory of life of the other'.

The answer to the legalism of the Jew is,
Christ died for us;
and to the licence of the Greek it is,
We must die with Christ.

Religious belief is not enough; there must be moral change. It is the discrepancy between our profession and our experience that needs looking to; and we must deal with it, not in the twilight of past attainment, but in the noontide of divine possibility.

The Christ who dying did a work *for us,* now lives to do a work *in us,* and if I understand the innermost significance of revival, it is, first of all, the up-filling of the divine life in the soul's experience, and then, the overflowing of that life in sacrificial service.

And now we come to the second point, namely,

EXPERIENCE

Every superstructure must have a foundation, but every foundation should have a superstructure; and *revelation* and *experience* stand much in this relation to one another. Experience which does not rest on revealed truth is bound to mislead, and may easily prove fatal; and a knowledge of revealed truth which does not find embodiment in joyful experience, leaves men cold, and often makes them cruel.

We should ever remember that doctrine is not the *measure* of experience, but is only its *mould*: and we must remember also, that experience is not the *standard* of truth, but is only its *apprehension* and *appropriation*.

In considering this matter of experience, let us turn to spiritual biography, in which, happily, we are rich, and let us see there the God of power, and the power of God, at work in the lives of His people, and learn how 'fragile vessels of clay' have held the treasure which has shown forth the divine excellency.

It should encourage us to know that there have been individuals in all ages who have entered into the experience of the *life more abundant,* and these have been persons of great diversity of temperament, and of every variety of accomplishment; and happily for us, some of them have spoken and written of God's dealings with them.

I am not now referring to what we speak of as *conversion,* but to an experience beyond that, and in many cases entered into long after it.

JOHN HOWE, in 1689, wrote on the blank page of his Bible in Latin these words:

> 'I long, seriously, and repeatedly thought with myself that besides a full and undoubted assent to the objects of faith, a vivifying, savory taste and relish of them was also necessary, that with a stronger force, and more powerful energy, they might penetrate into the most inward centre of my heart, and there, being most deeply fixed and rooted, govern my life'.

And then he tells us how he himself entered into such a blessing.

So was it also with PASCAL who, in a paper which has been called 'one of the most seraphic productions of human language', describes his exalted experience, and in a tide of love and ecstasy cried, 'joy, joy; tears, tears!'

The spiritual autobiography of Madame GUYON may be open to criticism in some aspects of its teaching, but no one can rise from the study of it without feeling that he has been face to face with God, and has had a vision of the believer's unlimited possibilities in Christ.

Looking for Christ in the depths of consciousness may, no doubt, expose one to serious perils, and while it is better, with SAMUEL RUTHERFORD, to go out of oneself and find Christ on the Throne, yet, the way of the mystic is not a forbidden way, and surely it must be the right way for everyone who arrives. There is no one prescribed way into fulness of blessing, provided that the blessing we desire and pursue has for its beginning, middle, and end Christ Himself; and it was Christ whom this devout woman sought, found, and enjoyed.

But we have illustrations of the truth before us far removed from the quietism of Madame Guyon.

GEORGE WHITEFIELD bears testimony that with prolonged prayer and self-mortification he definitely sought fulness of blessing, and there was a day and an occasion on which he received what he sought; when, yielding himself wholly and forever to Christ, he obtained the power which made his ministry an epoch-making thing.

Then, there is the case of JONATHAN EDWARDS whose ministry has been so potent on both sides of the Atlantic. This man, great of intellect and eloquence, tells of an experience of blessing into which he entered subsequently to his conversion. The year was 1737, and he went into a wood for quiet contemplation and prayer, and of what happened he says:

> 'I had a view that was for me extraordinary, of the glory of the Son of God, as Mediator between God and man, and His wonderful, great, full, pure, and sweet grace and love, and meek and gentle condescension. . . . The Person of Christ appeared ineffably excellent, with an excellency great enough to swallow up all thought and conception—which continued, as near as I can judge, about an hour; which kept me a greater part of the

time in a flood of tears and weeping aloud. I felt
an ardency of soul to be, what I know not otherwise how to express, emptied and annihilated; to lie
in the dust and be full of Christ alone; to love Him
with a holy and pure love; to trust in Him; to live
upon Him; to serve Him; and to be perfectly
sanctified and made pure with a divine and
heavenly purity'.

Coming from such a man as President Edwards
this testimony cannot lightly be put aside. The
Spirit of God took possession of him in such a way as
to fit him to be the means of one of the mightiest
revivals of all time.

Then there is DAVID BRAINERD, whose intimacy
with God was such that the record of it has made his
diary a religious classic, through the reading of which
William Carey, Henry Martyn, and *Robert Murray
McCheyne* were led to fuller consecration of life and
service.

Further illustrations of the experience of the New
Testament revelation of God's purpose for His people,
with which we began, may be found in the records of
*William C. Burns, James Brainerd Taylor, Charles G.
Finney, Frances Ridley Havergal, G. V. Wigram, William
Haslam, John Tauler, George Muller, Charles Simeon, Count
Zinzendorf, Gerhard Tersteegen, H. W. Webb-Peploe, Evan
Hopkins, Charles Fox, G. H. C. Macgregor, Bishop Handley
Moule, Arthur T. Pierson, Andrew Murray, Griffith
Thomas,* and a host of others.

These people learned the secret of bringing attainment nearer to ideal, and experience nearer to possibility. They apprehended that Christ was their
Inheritance, and that they could possess Him to the
very limit of an ever-growing capacity; and this

experience is for each of us also; an experience which will not only clarify our minds, but also purify our hearts; which will invade the innermost places of the soul, cleansing our motives, and taking control of the very springs of our desire. This is what Paul speaks of as being *filled unto* (and into) *all the fulness of God*.

Too many people have had an experience of the infilling of the Holy Spirit, and of a baptism of power, to allow of the matter being seriously called into question. If one's theology is sound it will not contradict the deepest experiences of the human heart.

Here and now anyone who will, can enter into this fulness of life, with or without emotion; intelligently, calmly, and deliberately by faith.

All Christians have what the New Testament calls 'eternal life', for without this one cannot be a Christian, but all Christians have not entered into the experience of abounding life. There can be relationship without fellowship; there can be life without health; there can be privilege without enjoyment; and there can be movement without progress.

One may war and yet not win, may serve and yet not succeed, may try and yet not triumph, and the difference throughout is just the difference between the possession of eternal life, and the experience of abounding life; the difference between 'peace with God', and the 'peace of God'; the difference between obtainment and attainment.

Abounding life is just the fulness of life in Christ, made possible by His death and resurrection, and made actual by the indwelling and infilling of the Holy Spirit. It is not the will of God that we should be as fruitless trees, as waterless clouds, or as savourless

salt, but that we should fulfil the highest functions of
our Christian calling. Christ's promise is that He
will slake the thirst of all who come to Him, and His
purpose for those who come is that 'out of their vitals
shall flow rivers of living water'.

The trouble and tragedy is that the Church has been
content to live between Easter and Pentecost; on the
right side of justification, but on the wrong side of
sanctification; on the right side of pardon, but on the
wrong side of power.

The difference between the World and the Church
is in the relation of each to Calvary. But it is
not enough that the Church and the Christian
be on the right side of Easter, which has brought
us forgiveness and life; we are called also to the
experience of Pentecost, which offers to us abounding
life, life which is characterized by trust, and peace,
and rest, and joy, and love, and power, and victory.
We are as unable to live this life in our own strength
as we were unable, in the first instance, to save ourselves by our own efforts; but He who began a good
work in us can and will perfect it in all who yield to
Him.

A mechanistic psychology denies what it cannot
explain, but the joyful experience and witness of a host
of Christians, from the apostolic age to the present
time, has been that 'the law of the Spirit of life in
Christ Jesus hath made us free from the law of sin
and death'.

If one is living before Easter, the Christ of the New
Testament is not in his experience at all; he is spiritually
dead. If one is living between Easter and Pentecost,
Christ is in his experience as Redeemer and Saviour,

he has spiritual life. But not unless one is living from and in Pentecost is the Lordship of Christ a reality to him, nor can he enjoy spiritual health, which is holiness.

No one can but be impressed by observing the change which Pentecost wrought in the experience of the apostles! In the between-time from Easter to Pentecost two things characterized them: fear, and a lost sense of vocation. We see them first behind closed doors 'for fear of the Jews'. And then later, Peter, who had been called to high apostleship, said 'I go a-fishing!' and the others said, 'We also go with thee'. No one can live the abounding life who is in the grip of fear, or who has failed or ceased to believe that God has for him a programme of life.

This between-experience has been the trouble from the beginning. It is illustrated by Israel in the wilderness between Egypt and Canaan, and by Paul's subjection to self, between his deliverance from the guilt of sin, and his freedom from its power, as set forth in the Roman Letter. It is this that is taught by the apostle's threefold analysis of men as 'natural', and 'carnal', and 'spiritual'. The 'natural man' has not reached Calvary at all; the 'carnal man' is on the right side of the Cross, but has not reached Pentecost; and the 'spiritual man' has entered by Pentecost into the kingdom which is 'righteousness, and peace, and joy in the Holy Spirit.' The carnal Christian has spiritual life, for he is spoken of as a 'babe in Christ', but there is little or no spiritual growth. He is like Lazarus, who, though raised from the dead, was yet 'bound hand and foot with grave clothes' until deliverance came. Is not this sadly illustrative of the experience of many

Christians, people who are in bondage to fear, or
doubt, or self, or sin? Yet freedom is our inheritance;
we are called to the liberty of the sons of God.

It will be a great day for each of us when we peni-
tently acknowledge that we have not been what it has
been God's purpose to make us; and it will be a greater
day when we dare to believe that we may become all
that it is in His power to make us.

We need not wait for Him. He is waiting for us.
In this place and moment He is offering Himself to us
as the source of strength and satisfaction, as well as
the place of safety, and if we will but receive Him,
fear will be exchanged for trust, doubt for certainty,
ineffectiveness for success, defeat for victory, and sad-
ness for joy. We have tried trying and have failed;
why not now try trusting? We have wrought in our
own strength and have found it to be weakness; why
not now take hold of His strength? The faith we
once exercised for the possession of divine life, let us
now exercise for the experience of abounding life;
and as Christ met us then, so will He meet us now.

And this brings us to the third point, namely,

SERVICE

Spiritual blessings are not vouchsafed to us for
selfish indulgence, but for sacrificial use. And, let us
understand, the quality of our usefulness will always
depend on the state of our heart. Our compassion
for men will be determined by our experience of the
love of Christ, and our appropriation of the divine
resources.

JOHN TAULER, great theologian and eloquent

preacher that he was, did not rise to the full height and grandeur of his calling until after he had retired from his pulpit for two whole years to seek in retirement that spiritual enduement to which he had hitherto been a stranger.

And D. L. MOODY bore witness once in Glasgow to such a crisis in his own life and ministry. He cried to God for power, and this, in his own words, is what happened.

> 'Well, one day in the City of New York, oh what a day! I cannot describe it; I seldom refer to it; it is almost too sacred an experience to name; I can only say, God revealed Himself to me, and I had such an experience of His love that I had to ask Him to stay His hand.
>
> 'I went to preaching again. The sermons were not different; I did not present any new truths, and yet hundreds were converted. I would not be placed back where I was before that blessed experience if you would give me all Glasgow'.

We all know now how far-reaching have been the results of that experience, throughout Great Britain and the United States, and literally throughout the world. For a restatement of this read, *The Second Evangelical Awakening in Britain,* by Edwin Orr, and maybe smouldering embers will be fanned again into flame.

It was so also with DAVID BRAINERD who 'in the shade and the cool wind' was wet with sweat as he prayed, 'drawn out very much for the world'; and grasping for multitudes of souls, so preached that scores of stolid, hard-hearted Indians were bowed like grass before the mower's scythe.

Temperamental gifts determine much, yet the Scriptures lead us to believe, and many saints bear witness to the fact, that each of us, much more than ever yet, may be conformed in inward experience to our outward standard, and may so know Christ as to be at all times among men 'the great power of God'.

Why tarries the much needed and longed-for visitation of grace? Perhaps if we look into our own hearts we shall find it is because we have as yet failed to comply with the divine conditions.

Can I ever forget the time, long ago, when my whole life and ministry were suddenly challenged; when it was revealed to me that I was little more than a middleman between my books and my people; when it dawned upon me that I was more anxious to be a *preacher* than to be God's *messenger;* that my master-passion was not the accomplishment of the will of God at any cost, and that my ruling motive was not the love of Christ?

In that hour the edifice I had been building lay in ruins about me, and for a while all was dark despair. But 'into the wood my Master came', and finding me there, in His mercy He brought me out, out into newness of life, out into fulness of service; and although I blush to think of much that lies between that hour and this, yet I gratefully bear testimony that His coming then and in that way, has been the determining factor of my life.

These, indeed, are solemn times, and the only hope of a distraught and disillusioned world, a world in which moral standards have been lowered in all directions, and in which greed of gain has taken the place of loyalty and goodwill, a world in the grip of a fear

that will not be smothered by gaiety and frivolity—
the only hope of such a world is a mighty and universal
movement of the Spirit of God, in and through the
Christian Church.

Is such a movement possible? *We* must give the
answer, not in words, but in a dedication of ourselves
to God, so complete as to checkmate the designs and
devices of the devil, and bring all the concoctions of
evil to confusion.

> Thy Holy Spirit, Lord, can give
>   The grace we need this hour,
> And while we wait, O Spirit! come
>   In sanctifying power.
>
> O Spirit of faith and love
>   Work in our midst, we pray!
> And purify each waiting heart,
>   Baptize us with power to-day.

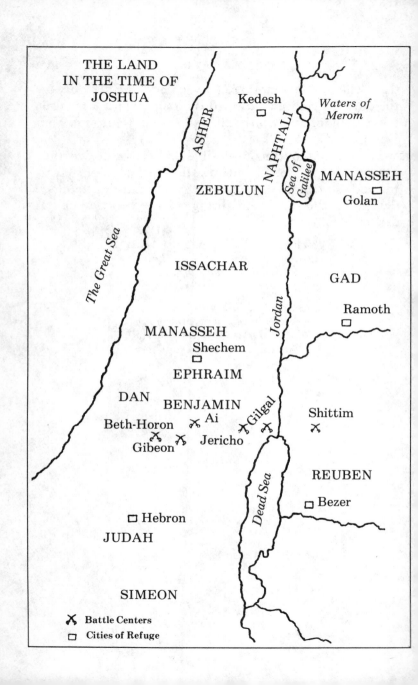

THE LAND
IN THE TIME OF
JOSHUA

ASHER

Kedesh

NAPHTALI

*Waters of
Merom*

ZEBULUN

*Sea of
Galilee*

MANASSEH

Golan

ISSACHAR

GAD

Ramoth

Jordan

MANASSEH

Shechem

EPHRAIM

DAN

BENJAMIN

Gilgal

Shittim

Beth-Horon

Ai

Gibeon

Jericho

The Great Sea

Dead Sea

REUBEN

Hebron

Bezer

JUDAH

SIMEON

✗ Battle Centers
□ Cities of Refuge